He Never Let Go

The true story of the evangelist who stopped believing in God

Lynda Alsford

StH
Seeking the Healer

All Scripture quoted is from THE HOLY BIBLE, NEW INTERNATIONAL VERSION®, NIV® Copyright © 1973, 1978, 1984, 2011 by Biblica, Inc.™ Used by permission. All rights reserved worldwide.

ISBN 978-1-326-51969-8

This version
Copyright© 2015 by Lynda Alsford
The right of Lynda Alsford to be identified as the Author of the Work has been asserted by her in accordance with the Copyright, Designs and Patents Acts 1988.

The names of some individuals in this book have been changed.

The painting used on the front cover is 'Sketch for the prodigal daughter' by Charlie Mackesy and is used with kind permission of the artist. ©copyright Charlie Mackesy www.charliemackesy.com

StH
Seeking the Healer

To all those who have been lost in broken dreams.
I pray you have the courage to allow Jesus to be your healer as I am learning to allow Him to be mine.

Contents

Preface vi

Introduction 1

1 Living a lie 3

2 My beginnings 12

3 Growing in Christ 26

4 The call to ministry 43

5 Being an evangelist 52

6 Addicted 64

7 Moving on 68

8 Lost in broken dreams 72

9 Doubt settles in 90

10 Adjusting 104

11 Newton's Cradle 109

12 Missing God 113

13 Reasoning 121

14 A wider search 133

15 Rediscovering faith 142

16 An old, new christian 149

17 Doubt: friend or foe 152

18 Church: support or idol 156

19 Why me? 163

20 Being not doing 174

21 Love and freedom 181

Also by this author 190

About the author 191

Preface

They (whoever they are) say that everyone has at least one book in them. Well, this is one book that I never imagined I would write. I never dreamed I would experience the things I have written about in this book. But then life has a way of throwing unexpected things into our paths. Having come through my experiences I want to share what happened to me so that it might help others going through a similar thing, or at least help those who know someone going through it. I leave the reader to be the best judge of whether or not I have achieved my aim. What I have written in this book is by no means meant to be a full theological discussion of any of the issues raised. It is simply a record of my thoughts at the time of my crisis of faith. As such the thoughts may appear incomplete to those really thinking the issues through for themselves. Any woolly thinking or unclear theology is down to me and all mistakes are my own.

At first, I told only a few people what happened to me. Then I started to wonder in April 2011 if I should write a book about it all. This meant telling more people to test out how they reacted to my story. So gradually, I started to share with my friends what had happened in my life and one of those friends was Kathie Kearney. She told me outright I should write a book about it without my having said it was in my mind. She was the first person to encourage me in this way. It confirmed to me I should get on and write my story down. Kathie, I needed your encouragement to get going. Thank you.

There are many others who have helped along the way. I hope I haven't missed anyone out. Apologies if I have. I owe a big debt of gratitude to Tim Ross, Dinah Alsford, Deborah Sutton, Patricia Francis, Andrew Wooding, Ali Hull and Richard Goode for reading various parts, and sometimes all, of the book through for me checking for mistakes. Thank you to you all. Also, a big thank you to Ali Hull for great advice about how to restructure the book while we were on an Association of Christian Writers weekend away at Scargill House. Also thank you to Rob Chidley for various emails of advice along the way. I am indebted to the Facebook group for the Association of Christian Writers whose members at times have helped with various queries about grammar or publishing.

I give a huge thank you to Charlie Mackesy for kindly agreeing to let me use his picture on the book's cover. Do yourselves a favor and check out more of Charlie's work, which you can do by visiting his website[1]. Also go to the Holy Trinity Brompton website[2] and look up his various talks in their 'talks' section. Not only can he paint and sculpt but he also speaks a great deal of sense about God.

I offer a big thank you to all the numerous people who encouraged me and prayed for me as I wrote *He Never Let Go*, whether though Facebook, Twitter, over the phone or

---

[1] www.charliemackesy.com

[2] http://www.htb.org/media/speaker/Charlie+Mackesy

face to face. You are all wonderful. At times I so needed the encouragement and prayer support you gave.

Lastly and most importantly, I offer an eternal thank you to God, Father, Son and Holy Spirit, for always being there. As Jesus said in Matthew 28:20,

"And surely I am with you always, to the very end of the age."

Lynda Alsford, March 2012

Introduction

If anyone had told me three years ago that I would stop believing in the existence of God, I would have laughed in his or her face. For twenty seven years I had been a Christian who was actively involved in the local church. I had also worked for three years as a full time volunteer in two different churches. Not only that but I had also trained for three years with Church Army at the Wilson Carlile Centre in Sheffield. From there, I went on to work as a Church Army evangelist in another two churches. At the beginning of 2009 I had been in my second post for eighteen months. I was working as the parish evangelist at Christ Church Turnham Green, a lively Anglican Church in Chiswick, West London. I was working with a wonderful team of people, who were friends as well as colleagues.

Under the leadership of the vicar, Rev Matt Boyes, I was feeling more confident in my ministry than I had ever done before. Matt was supportive and encouraging without leaving me feeling I had someone constantly looking over my shoulder. My work at Christ Church was going well. I felt I was achieving something. I had made good friends with people in the church. I was enjoying being in a local book club and a local sewing group. Given how well it was all going, having a crisis of faith was the last thing on my mind. Going through a time of not believing in the existence of God was not something I ever imagined would

He Never Let Go

happen to me, not even in my remotest, most awful nightmares. What follows is the story of what happened to me as my faith in God gradually fell apart before being gently pieced back together again.

1

Living a lie

"It's a lie. It's all a lie; don't believe a word of it. Believing in the existence of God will destroy your life."

These words were crashing around violently in my head like the proverbial bull in a china shop. The words were so insistent I thought I would burst if I didn't say them out loud. It was such an effort to keep them locked up inside me I could see the whites of my knuckles as I gripped the stand before me. I could feel my heart pounding away like it wanted to jump right out of my chest. I desperately wanted to make what was in my heart known to those in front of me. But I couldn't. I had to keep the words locked up, leave them unsaid, for the very good reason that as a part of my role as parish evangelist I was standing at the church lectern ready to preach a sermon.

It was just before 7:00pm Sunday, December 20th 2009 and I was standing in front of the congregation at 'Carols by Candlelight', the main carol service at Christ Church Turnham Green, in Chiswick, West London. I looked round the packed church trying to spot people I knew amongst the sea of unfamiliar faces. Although I could see some recognizable faces, I didn't recognize many of them because, as normal, there were a lot of visitors at the carol service. I felt alone and I felt distinctly unchristmassy. I tried to create a Christmas like feeling by allowing myself to be briefly hypnotized by the large number of candles flickering their golden and orange light over the room. I gave my head a minute shake, "Concentrate Lynda". The smell of pine from the big Christmas tree in the corner wafted towards me. No Christmas like feeling. I glanced at the nativity scene in the opposite corner hoping that seeing baby Jesus in his manger would make me feel more Christmassy. Nothing. I took in the sights, sounds, and smells that should have been full of the Christmas promise of love and peace on earth but I felt nothing, nothing but hopelessness and despair.

I had hoped in vain that the service wouldn't actually happen but after a warm welcome by Rev Matt Boyes, the then vicar of Christ Church, the service had started. I usually love singing carols like 'Hark the herald angels sing' at Christmas but this year, as we sang of joy and peace on earth, I couldn't have felt more different to the words I was singing. When Simon, a Church member, stood up to read the Bible, I thought, "Maybe this will put me in the right mood". I always love listening to Simon reading Scripture with his deep, clear voice sounding across the room. But not this year. I knew the words from the Old Testament book of Isaiah that Simon was reading very well but they meant nothing. Not even his wonderful voice could clear the gloom that was sinking gradually deeper into my heart with each Christmas carol I sung and with each Bible reading I heard.

This was the kind of traditional carol service that I

would otherwise love. I love candlelight especially at Christmas and I love singing Christmas carols. We had some of my favorites that year too. I'd joined in with singing about angels, shepherds, wise men and the baby in a manger. Along with everyone else, I had heard the prophecies from the Old Testament concerning the birth of the Messiah in Bethlehem. I'd heard how angels informed the shepherds of the birth of Jesus the Messiah and how Magi from the East came bearing gifts for him. This is exactly the kind of service that normally reminds me Christmas is more than presents and large amounts of food and drink. It normally speaks to me of the real meaning of Christmas.

But this year was not a normal year. This year I had been dreading it. I wanted to run out of the door. I knew I would have to preach at the end of the service and everything in me dreaded the thought of having to do it. As every minute passed in the service, as that moment drew progressively nearer, one more degree of panic settled firmly into my being.

All too quickly, it was time for the final lesson and I watched Peter walk up the step and stand at the lectern. Although I could hear the words that Peter was reading from an ordinarily much loved and well-known passage of Scripture from the first chapter of John's Gospel, it meant nothing. He might just as well have been reciting the alphabet. Then my breath caught in my throat as I heard the organist, strike up the tune for 'Silent Night' and everyone around me was singing that most beautiful of carols. It's generally the ultimate expression of Christmas to me. But now it was just another reminder of how different this year was. Almost before I knew what was happening everybody started to sing the final verse, and I heard people singing,

"Son of God, love's pure light, radiant beams from thy holy face"

This was my cue. I rose from my seat and walked shakily up to the platform to stand at the lectern. I didn't think my legs would hold me up.

"How did I end up in this position?" I asked myself as I walked up the step. "Why didn't I say no when Matt asked me to preach at this service? I should have simply told him I no longer believe in God and refused to preach".

Now I desperately wished that I had had the courage to do just that. However, I could see why Matt had asked me to preach at this service. I was a fully trained Church Army evangelist, and the 'Carols by Candlelight' service is very popular with those who are not regular members of the church. It made perfect sense that at a service attended by many non-Christians Matt would ask me, the resident evangelist, to preach the sermon. He wanted to make sure that those coming along to the main Christmas service knew the real meaning of the season being celebrated.

Matt had asked me to preach in the middle of a staff meeting one Tuesday a few weeks previously. One minute I was simply sitting there letting everything wash over me and the next minute this scary question had been dropped into the air without any warning.

"Will you preach at Carols by Candlelight this year?" Matt asked.

My whole body flushed hot and cold all at once as panic set in. My first instinct was to say no. I wanted to tell him how my faith was disappearing and I was no longer sure that there was a God. However, Matt wasn't the only one in the room. There were other staff members there too. I didn't want to tell everyone at once. I knew Matt's reaction would have been very loving and kind but I was uncertain that I would still have a job once the whole leadership team knew about my lack of faith. And that scared me. I wasn't ready for it.

On the other hand, I was unsure if I could cope with preparing such an evangelistic sermon let alone having to preach it. The thought filled me with such absolute horror I almost thought I would faint. I had seconds after he asked me the question to decide what I would answer.

I heard myself saying, "Yes". Fear of admitting my lack of faith to a room full of my colleagues had won the battle.

And now I was standing in front of the lectern at the carol service with a sea of expectant faces before me, all eager to hear what I, the so-called expert in evangelism, had to say. I looked out at them and wanted the ground to open up below me and swallow me up. I paused before starting to speak, hoping I would wake up and find out that the whole thing was just part of a nightmare. I didn't wake up. I had to open my mouth and start preaching. And I couldn't say what was in my heart. I had to lie. I had to pretend to be someone I wasn't. I had to say things I believed to be completely untrue.

I looked at my notes, took a deep breath, licked dry lips, and began to say the first sentence. I just did it; I was

He Never Let Go

on autopilot to a certain extent. It felt dreamlike, as if it was happening to someone else and not to me. I felt scarily disconnected from the person preaching so fervently on the platform. Out loud, I had started to preach the most passionate and most evangelistic sermon I have ever preached in my life. I had never before preached the Gospel in such a powerful way. I am sure some people there from the church would have been astounded and deeply shocked if they had known what was in my heart as I preached that sermon.

I felt as if I were being split in half. Outwardly, one part of me was preaching enthusiastically about the love of God shown by Him sending Jesus to die for our sins. But inside I was shouting out "It's all lies". Inwardly, all the doubts about God that had been building up over the last few months culminated at that moment in my being completely certain that there is no God. I don't think I realized just how far away from any belief in God I had come until I started to preach that evening. There was no room for maybes. I, the parish evangelist, had totally stopped believing in the existence of God. The pressure of being unable to speak out what I was thinking made me think I was going absolutely crazy. I don't mean that flippantly. I really thought I was at the beginning of having a nervous breakdown. I thought my soul was being torn irreparably in half.

I was a fully trained Church of England lay minister, and I had been working at this lively church for nearly two and a half years as their parish evangelist. In that time I had grown very fond of the congregation. They are a very loving group of people. I had seen them take up the challenge to open their church building to the public on weekdays for the first time. I knew that the people of Christ Church were committed to God and to showing the people of Chiswick the love of Jesus. If I had said what was in my heart that day I would have undone two and a half years of work. I would have devastated a lot of people and I cared about them all too much to do that. I had to keep my thoughts silent and keep on preaching what I had prepared, what felt like lies to me. Preaching that sermon is one of the most difficult things I have ever done. But finally, it was over. I had spoken the last words.

As I stepped down from the pulpit, I knew with utter certainty that I had to leave Christian ministry or I would lose my sanity. I had finally hit the crisis point a friend of mine had described to me some months previously. This friend had gone through the same thing I was now going through and told me that there came a point when leaving church ministry was the only option to prevent a nervous breakdown. Once I got to that point, my friend said, I would finally be prepared to face whatever difficulties leaving my career would mean. Until I got to the end of my tether a part of me had hoped I could make the situation work so that I didn't have to face the turmoil of leaving. I knew I had now reached right to the very end of my tether.

Working in full time Church ministry meant I lived in a apartment provided by my employer. It meant that when I contemplated leaving my job I was also contemplating leaving my home and completely relocating. It would be a huge upheaval. Until I stepped down from that pulpit on

He Never Let Go

December 20th 2009 the fear of change, the fear of losing both my job and my home, was greater than the pressure of continuing to live a lie. The 'Carols by Candlelight' service that year tipped the scales the other way. Now I knew beyond all shadow of doubt that I had to leave this job no matter what the cost in terms of possible homelessness and unemployment.

In the few steps from the pulpit to my seat, I made the decision to leave as soon as I could. My shoulders lightened. I closed my eyes briefly and breathed gently and slowly out. At least I now had something to aim for. All I longed to do was hurry home and comfort myself with a large amount of chocolate. However, I still had to face all the people who had heard my sermon over the after service refreshments. I still had to hide what I was thinking and feeling. My feelings about all this were so strong I thought someone would pick up what was happening to me. I felt as though I was walking round with a big arrow pointing at me with the words 'Lynda no longer believes in God' flashing in neon lights above it. But no one seemed to notice the big arrow. They did however congratulate me on what I had preached, assuming as they would, that I believed every word I had said.

"That's one of the best sermons I've ever heard you preach, Lynda" people said to me time and again.

Ironic isn't it? I had to stop believing in God to preach my best! If they knew what I was really thinking as I preached they would have been so taken aback. For the next hour or so, I had to keep up the pretence of being a Christian who loved every minute of the Christmas season.

The truth was that I was beginning to hate it. It reminded me constantly of my newfound lack of faith in God. This was the first Christmas I had experienced without believing in God. It seemed hypocritical to be celebrating something I no longer believed. As I socialized with people over the next couple of hours, it gradually dawned on me that I'd have to keep living a lie until I actually left and I had no idea when that would be.

I looked all around me and saw people laughing, getting into the Christmas spirit and enjoying the after service refreshments. Suddenly I felt completely adrift in an ocean of people who mistakenly believed I was a strong Christian. They all thought I was someone who knew there was a God of love and Jesus was His Son sent to die for our sins. A sense of extreme isolation seeped into my being. My heart sunk as I realized I still had to get through however many months it would take to leave this job. I already felt so lost trying to be something I wasn't. I didn't know how I was going to continue to live a lie. The decision to leave was a lifeline, but it had been thrown yards away from where I was. Somehow I had to get to that lifeline and I knew I had to do it as soon as I possibly could.

2

My beginnings

As I left the church that evening, I began to wonder how I had ended up in this awful position. All the way home to my apartment I thought through my life so far and what had brought me to this place. I got home and opened a large bar of chocolate, which was my main reaction when under stress. Overeating was a place of safety, a refuge and I used it now while I contemplated the situation in which I found myself.

It didn't seem possible that it had come to this. I started to question myself. Was my conversion real? Had I ever really believed in any of it? Had I been lying to myself for the last twenty seven years? I looked back over my life to see if I could work out why I had become a Christian in the first place. Why did I start to believe those lies I had just preached about?

I became a Christian at eighteen years old, about a month after starting my nurse training at The London Hospital (now The Royal London Hospital) at the beginning of 1982. Now I wondered why I had made that choice. What had happened to me that made me choose to follow a man who had lived two thousand years ago?

Looking back over my life now I've come back to faith, I can see how God has always had His hand of love and grace on me, although I wouldn't have worded it in that way as I left the Carol service that evening. Hindsight is a wonderful thing! So often when looking back, we see something we had been unaware of at the time. Don't you think it would be easier if we could have hindsight before events rather than after them?

As far back as I can remember, I have always believed in the existence of God. It was what I was taught as a child at Sunday school and as I got older, I became totally convinced that there is a God who created the world. I didn't know much about Him and I certainly didn't have a relationship with Him, but never did I doubt He was there in some form. I realize now that right from when I was a young child, God had been preparing me for the time when I would finally recognize and accept His presence in my life.

I was born at Brighton Maternity Hospital, in Sussex in the 1960's. I grew up in the county town of East Sussex, Lewes, which is situated on the river Ouse. It is also on the Greenwich Meridian, so is obviously due south of London. I lived with my parents Roger and Patricia, and my sister Deborah, who is two years younger than I am. My father used to teach Sunday school at Southover Church in Lewes and I attended Sunday school there until I was eight years old. Sunday school classes were held in the church hall which was down a little road opposite the church. It's a small cul-de-sac with flint and red brick walls lining the upper end of it. It has quaint old houses made mostly of grey and red brick.

I am sure that going to Sunday school down that little

road every week was vital in teaching me about the existence of God. The actual content of our lessons has evaporated in the mists of time, if I am honest, but they did leave me sure that there was a God and that Jesus was His Son. We were probably taught the usual stories. I've no doubt we learned the Christmas story of Jesus in the manger, angels appearing to shepherds and wise men following a star. I expect we learned about key Bible characters, like Abraham, Moses, David, Paul, and the twelve apostles.

One memory I have of Sunday school is being given a children's hymnbook, which had brightly colored pictures in it. The only hymn I remember being in that book is 'Praise my soul the King of Heaven'. I loved that hymn then and I still love it now. Now I find the words inspirational but back then I expect it was the lively music and plenty of alleluias to sing!

We stopped going to Sunday school when I was eight years old for two reasons. Firstly, at eight years old we were no longer in Sunday school but we had to go to Church services instead and I confess that going to church didn't appeal to me at all. Secondly, my parents divorced when I was eight years old and my father moved away. Given that Dad was the one who took us to Sunday school his leaving seemed to provide a natural end to our involvement with Southover Church. We saw our father only in school holidays after that. Every school holiday we would go to stay with him, his new wife Dinah, her two sons, my step-brothers, Peter and Jon, and later on my half-sister Caroline after she was born.

I may not remember much about Sunday school but I know I came away knowing there is a God and that the Bible teaches us about Him. I thank God for the loyal people who gave up their time to teach me the basics of the Christian faith. If you are a Sunday school teacher you are doing such an important job for the Lord. I know Jesus is delighted with those who faithfully teach children about God. Proverbs 22:6 says,

"Train a child in the way he should go, and when he is old he will not turn from it."

Sunday school teachers are training children in the way they should go. In all the Churches I have attended, there has been a core group of dedicated people giving up time to teach children about the truths of the Bible. They give up valuable time during the week in order to prepare lessons and then they miss out on the worship service themselves to give a crucial start in the faith to children. I even did it myself for a short while at one Church. Those of you doing this service are doing an essential work for the Lord. I pray God blesses you for your sacrifice in this area. I am eternally grateful to those who taught me. Even though I can't remember them now, something tells me I will know them when I see them in heaven.

All together I attended four schools. The first being the local state-run primary school[3], which I didn't attend for very long. The next one was a small private school

---

[3] In UK a primary school is for children from 4-11yrs old and then secondary school is for children over 11

He Never Let Go

called Lewes High School, which was in King Henry's Road. I was at this school from when I was five years old until I was twelve years old. One of my all time favorite teachers, Mrs. Monica Hecks, taught me at this school. Most of what I learned about basic reading, writing, and arithmetic I learned from this dedicated lady. I remember she had a little grey car that she called Grey Lady. Every year after I left this school, I had the pleasure of exchanging Christmas cards and letters with Mrs. Hecks (I could never bring myself to call her by her first name no matter how many times she suggested it!). I was delighted to be able to speak to her on the phone in the spring of 2011. She was in her nineties and still sounded so much like I remembered. Sadly, she has died since then.

Another teacher at this school that I remember fondly was a Christian lady called Miss Diamond and she taught me Religious Knowledge. I can remember her telling us about Jesus, about how important He is. I recall being concerned about those who had never heard about Jesus and I asked her what happened to such people. It struck me as unfair that someone should be judged according to something they had not been told. I remember Miss Diamond telling us that we could trust God to judge fairly. He would judge people according to what they did know, not what they didn't. Her assurances that God would be fair and not expect them to know something they couldn't know was important to me. Even at that young age it seemed essential to me that everyone was treated fairly. I had the pleasure of bumping into Miss Diamond at a Christian conference in the 1980's and enjoyed catching up with her. I was amazed that she remembered me and my sister Deborah.

When I was twelve years old I changed schools again. I was now going to attend Priory School, which was the local state-run high school. It felt rather scary at first. My old school was considered 'posh' by the pupils of my new school. Some girls from my old school were even bullied on their journeys to and from school by Priory School pupils. In one of the first assemblies at my new school, pupils were told off for bullying girls from my old school. This made me even more afraid of being bullied when they found out where I had previously been to school. Mind you, I didn't exactly help the situation. When the other kids asked me why I no longer went to Lewes High School, I said in my rather posh voice,

"Daddy couldn't afford the fees."

How to win friends and influence people! Not! I did however make a few friends, including Sue and Helen. It was because I knew Sue and Helen that I discovered my one saving grace as far as my new classmates were concerned. They found out that my grandfather was Lewis Turner.

Grandpa was headmaster of Pells Church of England School, which was also the primary school that Sue and Helen had attended before Priory school. Quite a few of our classmates were also ex-pupils of Grandpa's. He was a very popular headmaster. Sue and Helen said that he was strict but he was fair. Apparently he used to rap them over the knuckles with a ruler if they misbehaved (this would certainly not be allowed in British schools today but was considered normal back then). His strictness didn't seem to stop them having a huge amount of esteem for him. Being his granddaughter gave me at least some street cred!

I don't think I realized just how popular Grandpa was until his death a few years later when I was fourteen years old. It was trying to get to his funeral that really brought home to me how popular he had been. As was required, Sue, Helen, and I went to the school office to sign out of the school premises. When we were asked why we wanted to leave before the official end of the school day Helen spoke to the school secretary first.

"We want to go to Mr. Turner's funeral."

"No, you can't go." The school secretary told us firmly "Too many pupils have left school today to go to Mr. Turner's funeral. It's ridiculous."

"But he's my grandpa!" I was momentarily worried I may be prevented from going to my own grandfather's funeral.

"All right you can go but no one else is leaving school today."

When the three of us arrived at the church of St John sub Castro it was absolutely packed with people, including many of the pupils he had taught over the years. I felt proud that such a well respected and admired man was my grandfather.

Anyway, let's go back once more to a time not long after the beginning of my first term at Priory school. One day on the way into the morning assembly we were all given a New Testament by the Gideons International. It was a little, dark red book containing the New Testament and the Psalms. In the front of the book there was a list of various places to find help in the Bible and a list of daily readings. I started to read the daily readings in that little, dark red book and I remember the first book of the Bible I read back then was the Gospel of Matthew.

Although changing schools wasn't easy, I now thank God that I was sent to this school. Had I stayed at Lewes High school, I might not have received the gift of the Word of God. While I didn't make any formal commitment to God I did start to say the occasional prayer and importantly, I read His Word. I'm not sure I understood everything I read but I know it was gradually sinking into my being, drawing me closer to God. Hebrews 4:12 talks about how powerful God's Word is. It says,

"For the word of God is living and active. Sharper than any double-edged sword, it penetrates even to dividing soul and spirit, joints and marrow; it judges the thoughts and attitudes of the heart."

Isaiah 55:10-11 says, *"As the rain and the snow come down from heaven, and do not return to it without watering the earth and making it bud and flourish, so that it yields seed for the sower and bread for the eater, so is my word that goes out from my mouth: It will not return to me empty, but will accomplish what I desire and achieve the purpose for which I sent it".*

I know these Scriptures were true in my life. God's Word was beginning to accomplish in me what God desired. I was becoming more open to Him and more aware of His presence in my life.

Never forget how powerful the Word of God is in

reaching people. Looking back now I can see how essential having my own copy of the Bible was in bringing me to God. As the Scriptures I quoted above say, God speaks to us through His Word. Whether or not people respond to Him is not within our control but giving them a copy of His Word is. The Gideons International gave me the most amazing gift imaginable – the Word of the living God. They still work tirelessly to get the Word of God out to people who need it. How many hotel rooms, conference rooms, or hospital beds have people stayed in where there is a copy of the Bible in the bedside cabinet? The Gideons do amazing work putting God's Word into the hands of people who might not otherwise encounter it. I pray that God will continue to bless their work.

When I was fifteen my mum got remarried to a man called Patrick (Pat) who bravely took on two teenage daughters. Pat had a son called Nick, who is about three years younger than I am and he moved in with us as well. So, Mum gained a teenage son, and Deborah and I gained another step-brother. After the wedding we moved from Lewes to London to live with my step-father near the boarding school where he taught. Living in London was very different to living in Lewes in many ways. One of the first things I noticed was that London was much more multi-cultural than Lewes. People were different races and cultures which I found more exciting and interesting.

The second thing I noticed is that they didn't have the major bonfire night celebrations on November 5th as we did in Lewes. People from Lewes know how to commemorate the finding of Guy Fawkes with loads of gunpowder under the Houses of Parliament on 5th November 1605. This failed assassination attempt on James 1 is celebrated in style in Lewes. There are torch lit processions through the main streets of the town with people dressing up in all manner of fancy dress, accompanied by brass bands playing all sorts of music. A model of Guy Fawkes is set alight and thrown into the river Ouse with a flaming barrel. The people of Walthamstow East London didn't quite go that far. Not by a long way!

Another big change was that my new school, Walthamstow High School, was a girls' only high school. The school I had come from was mixed sex. Walthamstow High School was known locally as 'the green school' due to the color of the uniform. The school is within easy walking distance of Walthamstow street market, which is the longest outdoor street market in Europe. We would often visit it at lunch times. I settled in quite quickly despite changing schools halfway through my exam course.

Over the next few years I read my Gideon's New Testament often although not every day. Sometimes I would get bored and stop doing the readings but I was always drawn back to it again. I found great comfort in reading about Jesus. Every so often my reading of the Bible would be accompanied by prayers of desperation. I was a teenager and that is a difficult time for most young people but I also had to contend with severe acne. I had big, ugly, painful, red lumps on my face, back and shoulders, which made me feel like a leper. I imagined that people were staring at me everywhere I went; I felt so ugly.

He Never Let Go

I also couldn't sleep without being uncomfortable. Whether I was lying on my side, front or back I was lying on red, painful, swollen lumps causing me to cry myself to sleep, calling out to God for help. I had various treatments from doctors over the years but nothing really worked. Nevertheless, despite this or maybe because of it, the Holy Spirit was at work in my heart using the Bible to draw me closer to God. He was reaching out to me and He wasn't going to let me go.

By the time I reached my final two years of school, I had become friendly with a Christian girl called Lesley Hunt. She was a very faithful witness for Jesus. We spent hours and hours discussing the Christian faith. If truth be told, I never really took it seriously, thinking it was just a fun way to waste a boring lunch hour. It was a laugh, a joke. I would do my best to defend the non-Christian point of view and Lesley would speak for Jesus. I listened to her but never showed outwardly how much what she said was beginning to mean to me. With unbelievers I would sometimes argue from the Christian point of view, but I would never tell Lesley that! Take heart if you have shared your faith with someone. Many people will not outwardly respond to what they hear but the Word of God will have sometimes hit home and they might ponder on what you have said.

My lunchtime discussions with Lesley went on for the whole of my last two years of high school. She took me to a couple of evangelistic events during this time too. If my memory serves me correctly, Lesley took me to hear an evangelist called Eric Delve speaking at a *Youth for Christ* event. The truth I heard there spoke to me and a part of me wanted to respond to the message. I wanted to get up from my seat, go down to the front of the auditorium, and give my life to Jesus. However, anxiety about what my family would think and a fear of something new kept me from that response. I confess I never told Lesley at the time that I was touched by what I heard. Although externally I was not responding, inside me the truth of God's Word that Lesley had spoken to me over those two years was having its effect. Looking back, I am also sure Lesley prayed for me and there is great power in prayer. I wasn't completely aware of it but the truth was gradually sinking into my soul.

When I started to think about what I wanted to do after I left school initially I wanted to be a nursery nurse. I loved small children and wanted a career caring for them. However, I passed more of my final school exams than most people were expecting and the local college felt that I was too well qualified to do the child care course. Because of this, I rethought and decided to become a general nurse instead, with a view to going on to become a midwife. What I didn't tell Lesley (gosh what a lot of things I kept from her!) was that I had already decided that when I commenced my nurse training at the hospital I would probably become a Christian. The Word of God had touched me very much but fear still held me back. I think I felt I would be freer to go my own way once I left home.

I applied to various hospitals across London but the only one I was accepted for was The London Hospital (now

He Never Let Go

The Royal London Hospital) in Whitechapel, East London. My nurse training began at the beginning of January 1982, six months after I left school. I can now see that God had control of this situation too because I was training in a hospital with a very strong and very evangelistic Christian Union (CU). God had yet again brought me to a place where I would hear His Word preached. The CU at the London hospital was where I discovered my love of evangelism.

At that time, student nurses did all their training on site at the hospital and it wasn't then a degree course. We studied at the hospital school of nursing and worked on the wards alongside the qualified staff. Every eight weeks, there was a new intake of about thirty or forty student nurses. The CU organized a welcome party for every new group of student nurses. Of course, as is standard with much outreach to students, there was free food. There were also sketches performed, some of which were about nursing, designed to make them laugh but others were about Jesus. Then the CU president would give a presentation of the gospel message for a few minutes. After this the food was served over which we had discussions about what they had seen and heard. The CU president in January 1982 was a young man who was a medical student. I have now forgotten his name but I do remember that he suggested that we take the three years at the hospital as an opportunity to explore a relationship with God. I decided to do just that and started attending CU meetings whenever I could.

A month later sometime in February 1982, alone in my

room one night at about 11 p.m., I asked the Lord Jesus to come into my life. Having said that I think he was already present. In one sense I was just recognizing his presence in my life and accepting the salvation he offered. An enormous joy that I had never experienced before flooded through me. It seemed to come from deep within me. It wasn't a reaction to something external. It was an internal joy bubbling up from the depths of my being. I knew something extraordinary had happened to me. I felt I had to tell someone, so the very next thing I did that night was to write to Lesley and tell her I had become a Christian. I had never had such a quick response to one of my letters to her! She was absolutely delighted. Although I have kept in touch with her we don't see each other very often because she now lives across the sea in Northern Ireland, and I live in the South East of England. Nevertheless she is a very special person in my life because she was one of the main reasons I have the gift of eternal life. You don't get more special than that! God bless you Lesley.

3

Growing in Christ

Once I made the decision to give my life to Jesus, things went on pretty much as they had done before. At least I thought they did. I was wrong. I told no one, apart from Lesley, that I had made a decision to follow Jesus because I didn't think anyone would be interested. I certainly didn't think my decision had changed me in any way. However, one small incident demonstrated how wrong I was about that. One of the other student nurses in my group, Dina, who was already a Christian, noticed something different about me. She asked me one day as we were walking down Whitechapel Road,

"Have you become a Christian?"

"Yes, how did you know?"

She simply said, "I've been watching you."

Something had apparently changed and I hadn't realized it. I still don't know what it was she saw but I am glad she did because I then got more support in my new life as a Christian. If you are a new Christian, never doubt how thrilled other Christians will be when they hear you have turned to Jesus. It really does delight us as well as bring great joy to God in heaven. Jesus said in Luke 15:7,

"I tell you that in the same way there will be more rejoicing in heaven over one sinner who repents than over ninety-nine righteous persons who do not need to repent."

I didn't really change much about my life at first. Initially no one told me what was expected of me now I was a Christian. I simply kept on going to the Christian Union meetings on Monday evenings as I had done before. Mostly the other members were very friendly but I still remember feeling somewhat out of place at first. I heard people singing songs I didn't know and saw the joy in their faces. People prayed aloud. I had never heard people praying aloud outside of a church service before and then it was normally the vicar who prayed. It was all quite strange. The whole culture of being at a Christian meeting is so different from any other kind of meeting to which one might go. But it was here at this CU that I made new friends and was encouraged in my new-found life as a disciple of this carpenter from first century Palestine.

As well as learning a new culture of being a Christian, I was also learning my first career. I'm sure I had a fairly realistic idea about what nursing entailed when I started my training. I can remember being asked in my interview for the London Hospital School of Nursing what I thought nursing entailed. My answer was,

"Bedpans and vomit bowls."

I think that is a pretty realistic view of the job. However, I did start to struggle with my new role as a student nurse. There was so much to think about at once. I found it hard to settle into the job, especially having to do more than one thing at the same time, which is something I still find hard today. I know, generally speaking, women are supposed to be able to multi-task but the woman writing this book is almost completely incapable of it! I can only do one thing at a time. Any successful ward sister will tell you that this quality makes for a poor nurse. Good nurses can do quite a few things simultaneously and by this definition I was not a good nurse. I found it hard but kept on going. I hoped being a Christian would help me cope better with my career.

After I became a Christian I worked out that I should be reading my Bible on a regular basis. I knew enough to recognize that it told me more about God and I wanted to know more about Him so I started off by reading the only complete Bible I owned[4]. It was the one I was given when I was christened as a baby. It was a lovely white leather King James Version of the Bible with gilt edging to the pages. Not knowing any better I decided that because I started all other books at the beginning and worked through to the end I would do that with the Bible. I started with Genesis, the first book of the Bible and found this book was interesting. It is full of great characters, who were not 'holier than thou' but were as likely as myself to make wrong choices. It has all sorts of intriguing stories that match any of those in a crime thriller I might read. However, by the time I got to the third book of the Bible, Leviticus, I was somewhat bogged down by the various laws that are described. Starting at Genesis and working through to the end is definitely not a system of Bible reading I would recommend for a new Christian. Nor

---

[4] I still owned and read my Gideon's New Testament but it didn't have the Old Testament in it

would I recommend starting by using the King James Version of the Bible, unless you are already very familiar with it. My new friends told me I might be better reading a modern version of the Bible. I hadn't even realized that there were modern versions!

So, about three months after I became a Christian, I went off to a Christian bookshop near St Paul's Cathedral to look for a new, more contemporary version of the B4ible. I was stunned to see so many different versions. There were big ones and small ones. There were ones with pictures and ones without pictures. And there seemed to be so many different translations. Not knowing anything about the different translations, I didn't know which version to pick. I had no idea which translations are more like paraphrases, and which are more accurate translations. In the end, I bought a Good News Version of the Bible, which is written in modern English. It was therefore much easier to understand than my King James Version. The one I chose also had a front cover with a sunset on it. I love sunsets so I decided that was the one I wanted. I'm not sure now that choosing a Bible because it had a pretty picture on the front was the best way of choosing one but God worked with my odd Bible choosing system anyway.

Later, when my friends showed me their Bibles I was shocked to see that they had scribbled in them. Nearly all of them had underlined various passages that had particularly spoken to them. At first, it seemed like a rather unholy way to treat the Bible. But they explained that it helped them to remember what God had said to them. I

He Never Let Go

saw the sense in it and started doing the same thing to mine. I still have that Good News Bible with the sunset on the front cover. It is now thirty years old and is falling apart. Almost all of the New Testament and most of the book of Isaiah are now separate pull out features. It is pretty much held together with sticky tape. Nevertheless, I can't bring myself to throw it away, even though I don't use it much. This precious first Bible of mine has many verses underlined, which have spoken personally to me. I also have various notes about some of the passages written in the margins. It's a visible reminder of the early years of my Christian life and consequently far too precious to throw out with the trash.

If you are just starting out on the Christian journey I would recommend using a Bible in modern English. I would also suggest that you use a Bible reading guide. There are a number of these on the market and some are tailored specifically to new Christians. If that doesn't appeal then I would suggest starting with one of the gospels. Luke is my favorite gospel. It isn't the shortest but I like the way he remembers details about people. Luke was a doctor, so was no doubt used to taking personal information from people and remembering it. Reading a gospel will help you learn more about Jesus, who he was, and the things he did while here on earth.

Having a modern version of the Bible meant I found reading it even more helpful because I could understand even more of what I read. What I didn't know much about was prayer, so I didn't do a lot of it apart from asking for help with things that were happening (like coping with my work as a student nurse). I learned about prayer by experience as I went along. It took years to get to grips with it. I now think it would be beneficial to help new Christians understand more about prayer at the beginning of their journey with Jesus. I was simply expected to know about it almost as if learning about prayer happens by osmosis. It's just talking to God I was told but that doesn't help when you have never really talked to God before.

There is a book I read as a more mature Christian that I think is very helpful. It is called 'Praying through life' by Stephen Cottrell[5]. I so wish I had been able to read this book when I first became a Christian. It would have been so helpful, but it wasn't published until 1998. Stephen Cottrell makes prayer seem accessible to everyone. I highly recommend it.

As well as telling me about modern versions of the Bible my new Christian friends also encouraged me to go to church. They knew that the only churches I had attended before were Anglican churches at Christmas and Easter. Wanting me to feel reasonably comfortable with where I went to church they suggested two Anglican churches that many people from the hospital attended. The two churches suggested were, and still are, very popular with students in London. Either church would have been an excellent choice for a new Christian with a nominal Anglican background because both had, and still have today, excellent Bible based teaching and support for new

---

[5] Praying through life by Stephen Cottrell is published by The National Society and Church House publishing ISBN 0715149024

Christians. One suggestion was St Helen's Bishopsgate, and the other was All Souls, Langham Place.

So I began going to church at All Souls, Langham Place, near Oxford Circus because one of the people I knew also went there. The teaching there was excellent, with Richard Bewes, the rector, and John Stott, rector emeritus, being regular preachers as well as the various curates who also preached well. I am writing this chapter two days after the death of John Stott, so he is consequently on my mind. He was an amazing man. His preaching was very clear in content, style, and diction. He didn't mumble and he made sense in everything he said. I could always understand why he thought a particular thing, which helped develop my own thinking. I am sure that I know my Bible as well as I do because I spent the first five years of my Christian life going to All Souls, Langham Place, hearing wonderful preachers like Richard Bewes and the late great John Stott. It was a truly brilliant start.

At All Souls not only did I have brilliant teaching but also they had groups especially for new Christians, called beginners groups. They were there to help new Christians get to grips with the Bible, praying and living the Christian life. After completing a course in a beginners group, I went to a regular home group where support continued. The home group I attended was hosted by a man who was a great host. He sometimes cooked for us. His specialty was rabbit stew, followed by a rich homemade chocolate cake/cookie called Chocolate Crunch. I have very fond memories of that home group. After a few years, I went on to do a part time training year with All Souls called Core

Year, which was led by one of the curates. Again, I had excellent teaching during my time on Core year where we studied the book of Colossians.

One evening about nine months after I became a Christian I was sitting with a Christian friend, Pamela, in her room in the nurses' home. She went to a local Pentecostal church. I remember saying to her,

"I know I'm a Christian but I feel like something is missing."

This was the cue for a Pentecostal to give a talk on the Holy Spirit and Pamela didn't miss her cue! She sat down with me and went through the New Testament, teaching me that the Holy Spirit was God. She taught me that God, in the form of the Holy Spirit, wanted to live within me, to fill me with His presence. When she had finished teaching me, she offered to pray for me to receive the Holy Spirit. We knelt by my bed and she prayed for me. All of a sudden, I felt as if someone had their hand over my head. I glanced at Pamela and could see she had both her hands in front of her. We were alone in the room so I knew it was God. At that moment, it felt as though a fire had started to go through me. It started at the top of my head and flowed all the way through me. It was like having fire run through all my veins, right down to my toes. I just managed to say,

"I can feel it!"

Afterwards we were so giggly and happy. I knew I had had an amazing experience of God. He had come to me and filled me with the Holy Spirit. We went straight to our friend Dina's room and told her. She was delighted. Other

He Never Let Go

student nurses came out and asked what was going on. As on the very first day of Pentecost nearly two thousand years previously, they thought we were drunk. We assured them we were not drunk on alcohol but on the Holy Spirit. I think they thought we were mad. After that, I was much more aware of God's presence with me than I had been before. Something had dropped further down into my heart. God had become more real to me than He had previously.

One way in which God became more real after my infilling with the Holy Spirit was hearing Him speak to me personally. I don't mean in an audible voice but something deep in my spirit knowing that God's Spirit was communicating something specific to me. I had continued to find nursing very hard. As a result, I had started to doubt the rightness of continuing in nurse training and wondered whether I should leave and train as a teacher instead. I started to pray about it, wanting God's guidance on the matter. I talked about it to my step-mother, Dinah, who had also become a Christian recently as well as talking it over with my nurse tutor. At this point I felt I would almost certainly leave nursing but I wasn't totally sure and this is what I told both Dinah and my tutor.

One evening coming back from a meeting at church by underground train I started to flick though my Good News Bible looking at the pictures (sad but true!). One verse in 1 Corinthians leapt off the page at me. Well, it appeared to anyway. The words of this one verse almost seemed to be written in bolder type than the rest of the page. The verse was 1 Corinthian 7:20,

"Each person should remain in the situation they were in when God called them."

I knew I was taking this verse out of context but I also knew beyond all shadow of doubt that God was talking to me personally about my situation. I had to stay in nurse training. I received a letter from Dinah very shortly after that saying the same thing but using different Bible verses. Dinah's letter confirmed to me that God had spoken to me individually. It was the first time I had experienced the voice of God in my life in such a clear way. It was a wonderful thing to know that God Himself had spoken to me. I went to see my tutor straight away. I bounced joyfully up to her and said that I no longer wanted to leave nursing because God had told me to stay, wasn't that wonderful? She didn't know how to respond!

When I shared about being filled with the Holy Spirit at my beginners group at All Souls, I immediately got the impression that it was not something the leaders of the group agreed with. This was the first time I realized that not all Christians believed the same things about their faith. As far as I was concerned I had learned about the Holy Spirit from the Bible and had experienced it myself. Therefore, as far as I could make out, it was from God. It hadn't even occurred to me that they would not agree with it, but from then on I learned not to talk about my experiences with the Holy Spirit in certain situations.

Fortunately, my dad and step-mum were people who did understand. They had become Christians and we went together to Bible camps run by an Anglican minister called Colin Urquhart and his team at Kingdom Faith Ministries.

He Never Let Go

These Bible camps were a weeklong conference of Bible teaching and lively worship. I got a lot of encouragement from these camps although I can't say I enjoyed the camping part of them. I like my creature comforts too much.

Colin Urquhart and Kingdom Faith Ministries are charismatic, which means they believe that the gifts of the Holy Spirit mentioned in the New Testament are available for Christians today. They were the ideal place for me to be encouraged in understanding of the fullness of the Holy Spirit that I had experienced through my friend Pamela's prayer.

Some people receive something called the gift of speaking in tongues when they are first filled with the Holy Spirit. The gift of speaking in tongues is a kind of secret prayer language that God gives some people to encourage us. By secret I mean that the person praying in this prayer language doesn't actually understand the words they are saying. It is God praying through us by the Holy Spirit. It edifies our faith because we are praying as God would pray. However, given that others won't understand the language, we are told in 1 Corinthians not to use it in public worship unless someone is present who can interpret it (Interpretation of tongues is another gift that we may get from the Holy Spirit). I didn't receive this gift of speaking in tongues when I was filled with the Holy Spirit and I wanted it, if I'm honest, because a lot of my new friends had it. So I spoke about it to a friend of mine, who I knew did speak in tongues. She prayed for me to receive the gift.

"If you only have one word of a strange tongue in your

mind to speak," she said, "then speak it out to God."

"But it's just gobbledygook" I said, "I'm making it up".

She reassured me that it was unlikely I was just making it up. I tried again later in my room. I spoke the few words out to God and asked Him to take the words away if they were not from Him. It was just a few words at first but in my spirit I knew they were from God. This soon developed into many more words.

I am glad to have the gift of speaking in tongues because I find it a very valuable way of praying. I use it when I want to praise God but I've run out of words to use. Do you ever feel that you want to describe something but the words just won't come out? There don't seem to be enough words to describe what you are feeling. When I feel like that about something I want to pray about, whether it's something good or something painful, I use the gift of speaking in tongues. Alternatively, I pray in tongues if I want to pray about something but I don't know how to pray about it. Being able to pray in tongues is helpful at those times, but as St Paul says in 1 Corinthians 14, it is not the most important of the gifts of the Holy Spirit. In 1 Corinthians 14:2-3 Paul says,

"For anyone who speaks in a tongue does not speak to people but to God. Indeed, no one understands them; they utter mysteries by the Spirit. But the one who prophesies speaks to people for their strengthening, encouraging and comfort."

The gifts that are more important are those that edify others, not the ones that edify only ourselves.

He Never Let Go

Over the next few years I continued to study nursing and became more secure in my Christian faith. I also joined the team in the Christian Union who did the evangelism to the new student nurses. Our 'Set welcome' had been very helpful to me, stimulating my thoughts about God and giving me the courage to put into practice my desire to become a Christian. I wanted to help others get to the same point. In one sketch we did for the new nurses we made up a fake nurse's hand over report. It was supposed to be a night nurse handing over to the day shift. The nurse read out the name of each person on this imaginary ward, along with what was wrong with him or her. We had great fun with that sketch. The condition and treatment of one patient on this fictional ward was reported totally in abbreviated medical slang. The newcomers had no idea what it meant except it was a long list of various letters, which to them were meaningless. After the sketch we would reassure the new nurses that they would also understand it all sooner than they might imagine. We also had various sketches about our faith as Christians as well. I loved doing these welcome parties for people. It's where my love of evangelism started.

The first time I took my nursing exams I failed one of the papers and had to retake it. I was told that receiving a thin envelope with my results letter meant I had passed while receiving a thick envelope meant I had failed because it also contained the 'what to do now you have failed' papers. My heart sunk when I received a thick envelope. Later on in the pub my sister Deborah said to me,

"You're coping with failing because God is with you aren't you."

I hadn't noticed that was the case until she pointed it out. I just knew God was in control of my life and even if I messed up He would help me out. I retook my exams and once more waited for the results. On the day they were due to arrive, I remember sitting in the doorway of the kitchen staring at the letter box from quite early in the morning. Eventually after what felt like eons of time the letter dropped onto the door mat. It was a thin envelope. I knew I had passed without opening it and I ran down the hall shouting "It's thin!" rather than "I've passed". I found a job as staff nurse in the X-ray department where I worked for 6 months before moving to Reading, Berkshire to start an eighteen month course in midwifery. I thought I really wanted to be a midwife.

However, that wasn't to be. I can remember sitting in the first lecture we ever had as student midwives. I knew before the end of that lecture that I would never finish the course. I don't know if it was God speaking to me or if it was just my own knowledge of myself. Maybe I had so long wanted to be a midwife that the only way God could convince me that I didn't was by letting me experience it. I knew within half an hour of the first lecture I had made a mistake in doing midwifery. It took me three months to give in and leave though. I didn't want to admit defeat and failure but in the end I became so unhappy I had to leave. However, I did deliver 15 babies before I left, which is a useful thing to know in case of an emergency. Fortunately I have never had to use this skill.

He Never Let Go

At this point in my life I left nursing completely. I found it a constant struggle and decided to get a job as a nanny instead. So in November 1986 I found myself a job as a live-in nanny with a family in Hammersmith, West London, looking after two small children. I also decided I wanted to go to a more local church rather than going up to central London to keep going to All Souls Church. I started attending West End Baptist Church, which was just a few minutes' walk from where I was living.

It was while I was working as a nanny in West London that I entered another stage of my Christian life because it was here that I was baptized. Christian denominations have differing views about baptism. In the Anglican tradition babies can be baptized (baptism is another word for Christening) when they are still quite small. It is referred to as infant baptism. Three people (traditionally two the same sex as the child and one the opposite sex) act as godparents. The godparents' role, along with that of the parents, is to ensure the child is brought up in the Christian faith. Later, once children are old enough to take on the promises themselves (the minimum age is 11), they are confirmed, which is almost like a spiritual coming of age. It's a time when someone is taking on for themselves the promises made by their parents and godparents at their baptism. There is a special church service where the Bishop lays hands on them and prays for them.

However, some other denominations disagree with infant baptism. They believe people should only be baptized when they are old enough to own the faith for themselves. Babies in these churches are dedicated to God by their parents in front of their congregation. Once children are old enough to believe in the faith for themselves, they can be baptized. This is called believers' baptism.

In 1986, I started to feel that I wanted to make a public declaration of my faith. Up until then I had been going to an Anglican church, and had already been both baptized and confirmed prior to my conversion to Jesus. I thought there was nothing I could do as an Anglican in the way of a public commitment. As it happens, I now know I could have renewed my baptismal vows but at the time, I didn't realize this. During the summer of that year, I started to think about this more. As usual, I went to the Kingdom Faith Ministries Faith Camp run by Colin Urquhart. David Pawson, who is a well-known international Bible teacher, was there that year. He didn't agree with infant baptism but thought believers' baptism was more Biblical. Colin Urquhart is an Anglican and believed infant baptism was a valid form of baptism. One night someone asked them a question about baptism. I can't remember the exact question but think it was along the lines of wanting to know if people who had been baptized as infants were really baptized or not. That night Colin and David said they would go away and talk about it, rather than answering immediately and giving differing views from the platform. They felt it was important to give a united view. Later in the week, they said they thought it was between the individual and God. They suggested that one should pray about it. If, having prayed, the person believed their infant baptism was valid there was no need to be re-baptized. If, having prayed, they didn't feel their infant baptism was valid then they could be re-baptized.

In the months following that Faith Camp, I started to think about baptism. My family is nominally Anglican so I had been baptized as a baby and confirmed as a teenager even though at the time of my confirmation I wasn't a real Christian. I didn't believe it for myself. It was just something we did as a family. I realized that I felt cheated of a chance to choose to make a public commitment to Christ for myself. I began to share with the minister at West End Baptist Church that I wanted to make a public commitment of my faith, and that I didn't feel baptized. Well, you don't have to say that to a Baptist minister too many times before he has you standing in a large pool of water at the front of the church and in my case dressed in a long white robe. So, having had the necessary pre-baptism preparation to check I really was a believer, I was baptized by full immersion on 5th July 1987. It was a major step on my journey with Christ and when I came up out of the water, I felt God's presence in a way I had never done so before. I was grinning like a Cheshire cat and felt as though I was floating 6 inches off the floor! My baptism that day was a public declaration that I wanted to be totally committed to Jesus wherever He might lead me. I wanted to serve other people in His name.

4

The call to ministry

Little did I know that my call to full time Christian ministry would come so quickly after my baptism. I had often assumed that if God called me it would be to go to a developing country. I thought that because of my training, God would ask me to go to a place like Africa or Asia to work as a nurse. Secretly I dreaded it because I hate the heat. Even today I have a 'roll on winter' attitude when it gets hot here and by hot I mean when it gets over 23c/73f. See what I mean? I hate the heat. The idea of going to a place where it is very hot most of the time filled me with absolute horror. Many of my Christian medical friends had a 'burden' for India, Africa, or the Philippines. By 'burden' I mean that they knew God wanted them to go to a particular place to work because that one particular place always seemed to be prominent in their thoughts. I never did have a 'burden' for anywhere. I felt almost guilty that I didn't. I assumed that if I were used by God that it would be as a nurse in a very hot country. If God had asked me to do that I would have seriously contemplated deliberately disobeying Him. Ultimately I think I would have gone had God asked me to but I really didn't want to be put in that situation!

When my call to ministry came it wasn't what I expected. Within about a month of my baptism, Jesus had given me my first inkling of where He might be leading me. It was July 1987 and as was usual for me at the time, I had gone to the Kingdom Faith Ministries Faith Week. During the week a Christian pop group called Heartbeat performed a musical and visual presentation called 'Voice to the Nation', which was also the name of an album they released. It was all about how God is calling people to this country, to the UK and showed how much need there is here. The concept of Great Britain being a mission field for people wanting to be used by God was a new one to me and it excited me. I felt my heart stirring at what I heard and I knew then that I wanted to help those in this country. At the end of the presentation, the members of Heartbeat asked for people to come forward if they believed they were being called in some way to minister to those in need in this country. Hearing those words, I felt a 'spiritual nudge' and knew that God had spoken to me. By that I don't mean that I heard God in audible words but deep inside me I knew the Holy Spirit of God was speaking to me. I was up and out of my seat before I knew what was happening. Once I got to the front a lady, who was a member of the prayer team, prayed for me. I don't remember now what she prayed but as I went back to my seat, I knew I had been called to work for God in a full time capacity. What I didn't know was that it would take years before I was finally working full time in Christian ministry.

Over the following thirteen years, I tried various ways to find out what form of ministry God wanted me to do. I went to Bible College twice to help me seek the answer to what my ministry would be. The first time was in 1989 when I spent a term at Roffey Place in Horsham. Although I learned a lot there it didn't lead to any kind of Christian ministry. I guess you could say I felt like a failure. I had gone away to Bible College and had returned with no further details about my call to ministry.

I found myself returning to nursing instead. Returning to nursing is not something I ever thought I would do when I first left. However, so many people told me they thought there must be a type of nursing that would suit me that I returned just to make sure. I spent four years working as a staff nurse at St Joseph's Hospice in Hackney.

I discovered that I didn't really enjoy it on the wards any more than I had before. I found the wards very demanding and hadn't really learned a good coping mechanism for dealing with stress.

I was attending a local Baptist Church for part of my time at the Hospice. I found good people who I got along with and I enjoyed the worship. I was a part of midweek Bible study group with lovely people. My faith was strong but I can now see that it was not as deep as it could have been. It was a lot of head knowledge. I knew about Jesus and I studied the Word of God to learn more about him. But I don't think I had a deep intimacy with him, which looking back would have helped me more to cope with stress. It is a lesson I am still learning to this day – to allow my intimate relationship with Jesus give me strength for what each day brings.

I suspect now that stress is what caused the worsening

of a medical condition, endometriosis, which was to take 25 years to heal. Without going into detail endometriosis is a gynecological condition, which is characterized by a lot of pain. I had a couple of months off sick from work when I was first diagnosed and then struggled to cope with the pain in a busy job.

Instead of allowing Jesus to help me cope with this hardship I tried to carry on alone. I couldn't do it though and ended up turning to food to help me deal with it. I started to use food regularly as a way to deal with stress. I would go home at the end of the day and eat copious amounts of food. It numbed the feelings I didn't otherwise know how to cope with. I soldiered on with life, eating away the stress. However, a bright spot was now coming up on the horizon.

I spent my fourth year at the Hospice working in their Day Care Centre, which I enjoyed very much. In fact, when I went on holiday I even missed it and looked forward to going back to work! But despite this using food to push down difficult feelings had become a well established habit by now and it continued unabated. I was also still living with pain and seeking help from various doctors and hospital consultants.

During my time at the hospice I bought a apartment on the border of East London and Essex in South Woodford. I very much loved having a place of my own. I had a job I loved, a apartment and a car. Life was good but still there was something nagging away in my heart. I knew God had called me to ministry and I wanted to find out more about that call.

So, in 1994 I let my apartment out for a year and went off to Norwich to go to Bible college for a second time. I was there for nine months but once more it was no clearer what God was calling me to do afterwards. Would God ever speak to me more about the call He had on my life?

This time I didn't return to nursing but started doing homecare work instead. This work involved going into people's homes to care for them by helping with their shopping, getting them bathed, and cooking meals for them. I enjoyed this work. I have always liked people and it was varied work with interesting people.

It was while I was doing homecare that I saw an advert for a yearlong volunteer post at the All Souls Clubhouse, a Christian community centre in the northeast corner of the parish of my first Church, All Souls Langham Place. The job looked right up my street, so I sent off for the application forms. It was getting very near the closing date when the form arrived and I had only one evening to fill in the form. I prayed as I filled in the form and worked hard at it most of that evening.

I sent in my application and after an interview I was offered a place at the Over 60's day centre. I sold my apartment, moved into the Clubhouse, and spent a year living, working, and worshipping there. When I started there, they had recently been recognized officially as a place of worship and the Clubhouse was a church as well as a community centre.

I loved spending time with the older people there. Working at the Clubhouse confirmed that I wanted to stay in full time Christian work. When the year was up I wanted

He Never Let Go

to find a way to keep working full time in Christian work but as yet, I still didn't know what I wanted to do exactly.

It was then that one of God's amazing interventions led me to find out what my next step should be. While I was prayerfully considering my next step, two people suggested I might like to apply for one of the vacancies for lay assistant at All Souls, the main parish church.

I felt a familiar 'spiritual nudge' and I knew God wanted me to apply. I confess that I didn't really want to do the job. On the whole, the role was practical and involved a lot of cleaning rather than pastoral ministry. I wanted to work in a role with more chances to work alongside others in full time Christian ministry so I could learn more about that kind of work. When, as an act of obedience, I applied for the post I confess I was not best pleased to be offered an interview. I still couldn't shake the feeling that God was asking me to go to the interview even though I didn't want the job. I decided to attend it out of obedience to God. That is such a small phrase isn't it? Obedience to God. Easy to write but it wasn't easy to do. But I knew had to. So, with metaphorically gritted teeth I went off to the interview.

When I arrived the young woman showing me round handed me a slip of paper. She said,

"I shouldn't be doing this, but I have seen all the applications and I believe I should be giving you this. You have more experience than is needed for this role."

Then she handed me a small slip of paper that had been given to her by a lady who was a member of the lunchtime service at All Souls. This lady had asked that anyone not successful at the All Souls interviews might be given the piece of paper because her main church, in Streatham, was looking for someone to work as a full time volunteer Pastoral Assistant. However, this lovely young woman showing me round decided to give it to me before I did anything else that day rather than waiting and giving it to people who had been unsuccessful.

On the paper was written the name 'Rev Philip Mounstephen' and a phone number. In that moment, I knew without a shadow of doubt that being given that slip of paper was why God wanted me at the interview. He didn't want me to be a lay assistant at All Souls. I now knew for certain I wouldn't get the job at All Souls or if I was offered it I should turn it down. I also strongly suspected that I would be offered a job by Rev Philip Mounstephen, whoever he turned out to be. Later in the interview, I was asked if I had any other job opportunities lined up. I can't remember now if it was the church warden, or Rev Richard Bewes the then rector who asked me that question as they both interviewed me that day. Maybe they both asked me the question. However, when asked it, I looked them straight in the eye and said truthfully, that I did.

I phoned Philip Mounstephen as soon as I could after leaving the interview. He was delighted to hear from me. It transpired that he was vicar of St James Church, an Anglican Church in Streatham, South West London. One of his hopes for the work there was that they would find someone who would help increase the work with older people. St James Church worked very closely with

He Never Let Go

Mitcham Lane Baptist Church [MLBC], which was next door to them. The youth work at both churches was by then a combined work. Philip, together with the then pastor of MLBC, Rev David Whitlock, wanted the older people's work to be combined between both churches as well. So Philip was very pleased indeed when I phoned out of the blue and said I was looking for a full time volunteer post and that I had nursing, and over 60's day centre experience.

I soon found myself sitting in Philip's study at St James' vicarage in Streatham. The interview was with Philip and his curate Rev Cameron Barker. Philip offered me the job on the spot.

"This is only the second time I have made an on the spot decision like this," he said glancing at Cameron "In fact the only other time was when I employed Cameron, and I was proved absolutely correct then. "

I told him I wanted to think and pray about it for a couple of days. That makes me sound more spiritual than I was feeling at the time but I just wanted to be absolutely sure it was the right thing to do. After praying I felt that familiar spiritual nudge giving me the assurance that it was the right thing for me. I phoned Philip to accept his offer a few days after the interview, from a phone box on Southend sea front, while on a day trip with the over 60's day centre. As soon as I told him I was accepting his offer, he said,

"Now you have accepted I have to tell you I am leaving St James."

I only actually worked with Philip for about 2 months

before he left.

I spent two very happy years working at St James' West Streatham managing to achieve the task set me by Philip when I commenced working there. By the time I left there were quite a few volunteers from St James going over to MLBC to help with their over 60's lunch club, which was called Young at Heart. In fact a little while after I left one of St James congregation became the coordinator for Young at Heart. I had accomplished what I set out to do and it felt good.

5

Being an evangelist

After being at St James for about a year or so, I began talking to Cameron, the curate, about my future. In one conversation he started thinking aloud various options for full time ministry in the Anglican Church. One thing he mentioned was Church Army[6]. As he said the words Church Army, I could see an imaginary light bulb get switched on in his head. His eyes opened wider and he tilted his head slightly, making an almost silent "Mmm" noise. Outwardly he said nothing as far as I remember. When I questioned him about his reaction, in a typically Cameron like way, he said no more than suggesting I look up more details about Church Army for myself. In this way, having simply planted a seed, Cameron trusted God to do the rest of the talking to me. Cameron's strategy worked and I investigated Church Army. I liked what I saw.

Church Army's strap line is 'Sharing Faith through Words and Action', which today is normally written as 'Faith Words Action'. I loved that immediately. I had often been concerned when seeing people speaking the words of

---

[6] To find out more about Church Army visit their website www.churcharmy.org.uk

the gospel but not necessarily backing it up with action as well. I had always felt that words and action go hand in hand. In my opinion love is an action as well as a feeling. I believe that we can't tell people Jesus is Good News, if when they are suffering we do nothing to alleviate their pain when we can. Today I am even more convinced than ever we need to show people Good News in practice while speaking the Good News about Jesus.

The only thing I didn't like about Church Army was that the training centre was based in Sheffield. This was very bad news for me. Now Sheffield, as I later found out for myself, is a great city in which to live but I had lived virtually all my adult life in London and I didn't want to move away. All my friends and family are in the South of England and I didn't want to move away from them. As a single person living alone, all my emotional and spiritual support comes from outside the home. This makes my friends and family a vital encouragement for me. These fears of moving away caused me to doubt the rightness of Church Army for me. If I trained as a priest, I could do that in London, so I tried to convince myself that God didn't want me at Church Army. I am sure I wasn't the first person, and certainly won't be the last, to try to dress up my own desires in the voice of God.

Fortunately for me I had been discussing my doubts about Church Army with Cameron, who sensibly pointed out that Church Army's selection process was far shorter so it made sense to go through that first. He told me that the selection process for ordination was much longer and involved a lot more waiting. If Church Army didn't accept me, he reasoned, I could make the decision to try for the longer process of applying for ordination. Rev Cameron Barker is a very wise man. Had he tried to tell me something like 'God has told me you should be in Church Army, and you must not apply for ordination' I would have almost certainly done the opposite (very human of me I know but I am very human!). As it was, Cameron just pointed out how applying to Church Army first would benefit me more. I think we can often over-spiritualize decisions. I sometimes wonder if God is more practical than we are in these things!

So I applied to Church Army and my initial application was accepted. After that there were various interviews to go through. The first of these was in the form of a very informal visit to my home by Church Army Captain Ray Khan. In fact I think I was wearing my slippers for the interview! I liked Ray straight away. He was warm, friendly and a good advert for Church Army. He obviously thought I would be suitable because I got through to the next stages.

The final part of the process was a weekend of interviews at the Wilson Carlile College of Evangelism[7] in Sheffield. The other candidates and I would have five interviews over the course of the weekend. Two of these were with two interviewers, the other three with one interviewer. Some of the other interviewees gave nicknames to the various people interviewing us. One

---

[7] This is now Wilson Carlile Centre, which has a café and bookshop open to the public. Training is now based in various Mission Centers around the country.

interview was with the then principle of the college and the then college director of studies. Their interview focused on my ability to learn and study. They became known as 'The gruesome Twosome'. I think some found the interview with them hard going but I enjoyed mine. In addition to talking about learning I discovered that the principle and I had attended the same school.

The other pair of interviewers who acquired nicknames were Church Army's director of operations and a Church Army Sister who was working as an Evangelist in a parish. Their focus was spiritual life. Some people also found this interview hard but again I enjoyed their interview too. This pair of interviewers had two nicknames. One was 'The smiling assassins' and the other was 'The Rottweilers. In my humble opinion neither nickname was applicable to them. Well, actually the smiling bit of the smiling assassins was correct just not the assassins part. We were convinced these nicknames for them were secret. It never occurred to us that they would know them. However, one of the other interviewees told us that when he left his interview, the director of operations said to him, "mind your heels", and barked like a dog. Hearing this pleased me. I really liked his sense of humor.

A group of us went off to the local pub on the Saturday evening of that weekend. The local pub at the time was the Bath Inn and going to it was nicknamed 'going for a bath'. That Saturday evening I sat next to an Evangelist-in-Training called Vanessa whose husband Jeff was one of the other interviewees. She looked at me during the evening and said,

He Never Let Go

"You know you're coming, don't you?"

I had been trying all weekend to avoid the growing realization that I was going to be accepted into training but Vanessa was right. Something in me just knew I was going to be accepted even though I didn't want to leave London. I knew I would be returning to Sheffield the following year to start training. Two days after I returned home, on the Tuesday morning, I got a letter from Church Army. When I opened it I found a letter of acceptance inside. I burst into tears. And they weren't tears of joy. The thought of leaving all my friends and family was just too hard.

I had six months before I started training and there was a lot of grieving in those six months. The thought of leaving behind my family and friends was tough. Once more, I would have to start all over again. I think it is the thought of the loneliness that comes in the first few months that I feared most. There are different pressures in relocating when you are married with a family or when you are single. The advantages for me as a single person were that I didn't have to worry about anyone else. I wasn't concerned with children finding new schools and how a spouse would settle in. However, as a single person relocating I am completely alone when I get to the new place. For the first few months I spend all my days surrounded by strangers. There is no one with whom I spend time who has known me longer than I have been in my new place. A married person will go home to someone familiar. I knew I would not have that luxury.

Actually I can remember saying something similar to Philip Mounstephen when I first started working at St

James in Streatham. At first my day off there was midweek. After about three weeks I asked Philip if I could have a Saturday off that week. I said to him,

"I just need to have face to face contact with someone who has known me for longer than 3 weeks"

I don't think he had realized until then that as a single person I wouldn't have that in a new situation. Once I pointed it out to him, being the good man he is, he was very supportive and immediately changed my regular day off to a Saturday so I could get away to see friends and family on a frequent basis. However, Sheffield was much further away than going from one side of London to the other. I was nearly 200 miles away from everyone I loved. The fear of those first few months of isolation terrified me and as usual I buried my fear in overeating. Sometimes people told me not worry as there would be other single people there with whom to make friends. But I knew I would make friends eventually. It is the first few months while you are building new friendships that are so lonely.

In the six months prior to starting college all of us future evangelists-in-training also had a correspondence pre-college course to keep us occupied. There were also three visits to college for weekends of more pre-college study. On one of these weekends all the pain and grief of leaving London and starting somewhere new came out when I burst into tears on one of the admin staff. When they saw how upset I was I am sure they thought I would back out and not turn up when college started. However, once I did move to Sheffield I settled in very quickly. I think I did all my grieving before I left rather than after I

He Never Let Go

arrived in Sheffield.

I enjoyed my three years of training very much and was very settled there. I didn't struggle with the academic work and although I didn't get many A's (unlike some people in our year group who seemed to get loads), I didn't fail any modules either. I seemed to get mostly B's. I confess I was probably a bit lazy when it came to assignments. I worked out after my first year that if I worked really hard, slogged away at reading around the subject for days, and worked long hours on my essay I got a high graded B. If I merely did a little bit of work, and regurgitated the lecture notes I got a low graded B with a note on the bottom saying I had regurgitated the lecture notes. On paper they both look like B's. So I made a conscious decision to stick with my lazy way (apologies to any of my tutors who are reading this – at least I am honest!). There were some wonderful people in my year group and I really enjoyed getting to know them. They always made lectures lively and interesting.

I lived in one of the campus apartments during my first year and sometimes I longed to get away from college in my time off. I was still using food to deal with difficult emotions though and put on a lot of weight in the first twelve months.

However, in my second year I moved into a house with another student. I really enjoyed my time in that house and was settled. It gave me the strength to start to attend a local weight loss group. I lost a total of about 60lbs over the 2 years and felt better than I had done in ages. But I hadn't actually dealt permanently with the overeating problem. What I did was control it. I had a time once each week when I would eat unhealthy food – lots of it. The rest of the week I managed to eat according the diet plan and in this way lost the weight. I thought I had lost it for good.

I also found a lovely church, St Timothy's (St Tim's) in the Crookes area of Sheffield, with a wonderful vicar, Rev Phil Townsend. I found this church because Phil used to be a curate at St James West Streatham (some years before I worked there) and I was told about him and his church before I left for Sheffield. Being there was like having a connection with familiar people and places.

On my first visit to a Sunday Service at St Tim's, there was a sketch with the main character lighting up a cigarette during the performance. I was surprised as I had never seen anyone smoke inside a church building before, even if it was part of a sketch. Later in the service Phil used a water gun (actually it was more like a water sub machine gun) as part of a sermon illustration. He then proceeded to turn the water gun playfully on the people unfortunate enough to be sitting in the first few rows. When I told my friend Glynis at St James about my introduction to Rev Phil Townsend, she said,

"Phil hasn't changed then!"

I decided to make St Tim's my spiritual home. I appreciated that Phil didn't push me to get involved at all in the church preferring me to enjoy my last 3 years of being an ordinary member of the congregation with no pressure to be involved. He knew there was plenty of involvement with church life coming up later.

Phil was right. There were many church activities to be

involved with once I started my first post in London. I started my ministry in the parish of Holy Trinity with St Paul and St Mary in Hounslow, West London, which is about 5 miles from Heathrow airport. I soon learned to live (or not as the case may be) with the lovely background noise of airplanes going overhead! Joe, one of the students in the year below me at Church Army college, had come from Holy Trinity Hounslow. So while I was still considering the offer of working there I asked him what it was like as a Church. I was looking for a label such as evangelical, catholic, charismatic, high, or low because I wanted a way of working out what kind of worship and theology they had there.

Joe replied "It's high, low, evangelical, charismatic, and catholic."

"Mmm, that doesn't help, Joe"

However, once I got there I knew exactly what he meant. It didn't fit neatly into any label of churchmanship one might try to put on it. It was an amazing place (and still is!).

I spent 4 years at Holy Trinity, working as their parish evangelist in the Church's Bridge Centre, which was a coffee shop and bookshop in the front part of the church. One part of my role as Evangelist I enjoyed very much was standing behind the counter in the coffee shop meeting and getting to know regular customers.

Nevertheless, I also found church ministry stressful and very isolating. I met many lovely people but a lot of them knew me only in my role as an evangelist and related to me in that way. I could go weeks at a time seeing only people who knew me in that role. Sometimes I longed to have face-to-face contact with someone who simply knew me as Lynda, and not as Lynda the evangelist. I wanted to spend time with someone who had known me before I became one of the church staff. Having a day off in the week when most folk are working, and being on duty myself many weekends and evenings, is not conducive to close relationships outside the church. Being single, and living alone, meant I didn't even go home to someone who knew me outside of my role as evangelist. Restrictions on who I could have living in the house that went with the job meant I couldn't easily take a house mate but often jumped at the chance to have a volunteer lodge with me for a couple of months. Although ministry was hard I stuck with it.

When I first arrived in the Hounslow area I joined a local weight loss club for a few months but I didn't stick at it long. I didn't want to restrict my eating – it was still the main way I dealt with stress. I had lost weight yes, but I hadn't dealt with the reasons why I overate in the first place. So gradually, I started to put on all the weight I had lost. My smaller clothes had to be put away and I had to buy new bigger ones. I had given away all my 'fat' clothes having been so sure I'd not need them again. I was embarrassed and felt a deep sense of shame at my failure.

I was beginning to realize that weight loss clubs were not the answer to my eating problems. My eating was spiraling out of control and I was out of my depth in finding an answer. I used to think my being overweight was just a lack of will power, but in time I came to see there was more to it than the amount of will power I did or didn't have. I described it as being 'like an addiction' until I realized that it really was an addiction. I was addicted to food, in particular to sugary foods, chocolate and bread.

To this day, I can't pinpoint a time when a little comfort eating turned into major binge sessions. I think it was a gradual process over a number of years. I wish I had stopped before it got out of control but I didn't. I continued with my 'drug' use. In some ways I am grateful that it was food I chose and not heroin, alcohol or gambling for example. Those things are more immediately life destroying than food. Food addiction is easier to hide in some ways and on the whole it doesn't cause immediate problems. It is also the least damaging of the eating disorders too. Anorexia and bulimia produce more immediate health problems. Compulsive overeating causes long term difficulties once the weight goes on.

Why, though, did I choose to eat my pain away? I will probably never know the answer to that question. Some of us are apparently more prone to becoming addicted to things, although scientists vary in the reasons they give as to why this should be. Is it that we are born with a physiological reason for our brains to react that way? Or can repeated use of an addictive substance have that effect on anyone? And why do some of us chose food as an addictive substance while others chose alcohol, drugs or gambling, for example? I don't know that either but I do know that is what happened to me. At some point I learned that large amounts of food soothed my pain away for a short while. Once I made this discovery I kept eating to maintain that effect. In a way you could say I chose the captivity I suffered. God is gracious though and still helped me find freedom despite it being self-inflicted. His love knows no bounds.

A part of me was screaming out desperately to everyone who would listen that I needed help. I was in no doubt that I was an addict. I knew I needed help but didn't know where to go. But other people didn't share my ideas. Yes, people were addicts. They were addicted to gambling, drugs or alcohol but food...? Many people didn't think it was possible to be addicted to food. Sometimes it was a battle to keep on seeking for freedom against the tide of unbelief around my problem. I almost gave up on a number of occasions. Thankfully I didn't. I kept on keeping on.

On the positive side, my time at Holy Trinity confirmed that I enjoyed ministry itself. I grew in confidence with my preaching and teaching. I had good feedback from people, which encouraged me. I started a lunch time service, which was popular with volunteers and customers of the coffee shop. I loved telling people about Jesus and his love. I grew in confidence about my ability with people.

6

Addicted

One Good Friday during my time at Holy Trinity Church I had an encounter with God that made me realise how little I accepted myself. I became aware I needed to find out how God sees me and bring my view of myself into line with God's opinion of me. This excited me and I began to get a glimpse that the healing of my eating problem would come directly through my relationship with Jesus. I started now to feel far more hope in my search for wholeness in this area. I began to see that I had a hunger inside me, but I didn't know what the hunger was exactly. I simply knew that only God could satisfy it. I was also certain that food would never satisfy that hunger no matter how much I ate. From this point in my life onwards, I had far more assurance of my eventual liberty from this addiction.

Although I still didn't know how to go about letting God fill the need within me, I did at least have more of a direction than I'd had previously. God kept leading me onwards to my goal. One weekend I heard a speaker called Maxine Vorster. She had been healed from the eating disorder bulimia. She spoke about the need inside her that God had filled. Her very helpful story persuaded me that I was on the right track.

Maxine wrote a book called 'Hidden Hunger'[8], which I bought that day. I devoured it, finding it so encouraging to read in detail how she found freedom. The name of her book, 'Hidden Hunger', confirmed once again that I was on the right track. There was another hunger deep within me and God Himself would satisfy this hunger in me. This knowledge alone gave me huge hope. It reinforced the knowledge that I could be free from food addiction. It was yet another encouragement to never stop seeking freedom until I found it.

Step by step, I was moving towards a place where I could get closer to God. God, as always, met me where I was and led me kindly onto the next step in my journey to freedom. The next step I found myself taking was a vital one and I am forever grateful to God that I discovered the next group of people to help me.

A chance encounter with a young woman in the course of an interview for extra work introduced me to a group called New ID[9]. I discovered that New ID is a six-week Christian course for those struggling with eating disorders. It gives the message that freedom is possible. Not only that but it was being run here in London at Holy Trinity, Brompton. This co-incidence (or is that God-incidence) confirmed that God was with me in my search for freedom. I knew I was right to keep seeking release

---

[8] Hidden Hunger by Maxine Vorster ISBN-10: 1860245889, ISBN-13: 978-1860245886
[9] New ID is a six-week Christian course for those struggling with eating disorders, bringing the message that complete freedom is possible. For more information go to http://newid.org

from the captivity of my eating disorder. I knew that by going to New ID I would be walking one small step further towards freedom.

Although I was excited to go to New ID, a part of me was also scared. I guess I was fearful of the unknown but I needn't have worried. In my first meeting while I was browsing the bookstall an attractive young woman with long dark wavy hair approached me. She introduced herself as Mel Oliver, the course leader. She put me at ease and I started to relax.

Soon Mel warmly welcomed us all and told us it was a safe place, where we would find support. She told us that New ID could not guarantee or promise we would be recovered as a result of doing the course. The course was to make sure we knew that complete freedom is possible and to help us realise we were not alone. I was already feeling more hopeful about freedom and also feeling less isolated by hearing about the course and being there on the first day added to this sensation. Mel informed us that each week there would be a testimony followed by a talk. There would then be a short break before we divided into small groups for discussion. Sometimes the testimony and talk would be given in person by either Mel or a visiting speaker. At other times, we would watch the talks on a DVD. She advised us to stay in the same groups for the course if possible because it would help build relationships with other attendees.

On that first week, Mel gave us her testimony. She spoke eloquently from the heart about her own struggles with an eating disorder. As she described her own battle, I was amazed that this gorgeous woman in front of me had once been so bound by the chains of an eating disorder. Now she was free, she told us, completely free. I felt a surge of hope as I listened; it was like a spring of life-giving water rising up inside me as Mel spoke.

I went along to two meetings but the third one, called 'Dealing with emotional issues' was more difficult. At the start of the evening, Mel warned us that there is a drop off in numbers after that session because it begins to probe under the surface to the emotional reasons for our eating disorders. All kinds of emotions got stirred up in me and I suspect I blocked out some of the meeting. However, I can remember what I felt as I drove home. I was feeling extremely jittery and knew I couldn't cope with going home alone if I was not armed with loads of chocolate. I had a gnawing, almost painful, emptiness inside that I knew wasn't physical hunger but felt so like hunger that I had to eat. It was a deep dark hole in my soul that I knew would be filled by food, at least temporarily. I was scared that this hole would eat me up if I didn't eat food.

For a few moments the next day, I didn't want to go back to New ID. I wanted to walk away from having to deal with these nasty feelings. But I couldn't run away because I was going with friends to whom I had promised a ride, so I continued with the rest of the course. It was very helpful but it would be a long while before I could stand up and say I was completely free. But I was now even more convinced that freedom is possible and not only was it possible in a general sense it was possible for me too. I would be free one day.

7

Moving on

As my contract with Holy Trinity drew to a close I needed to find another job. I started looking for another ministry post as an evangelist but there are often only a few advertised. Every time I thought about the situation the lead weight in my chest got heavier and my pulse quickened. I wondered what on earth I would do if I couldn't find another job before I had to leave Holy Trinity. I scoured the Christian press looking for appropriate jobs. I found a few, which I dutifully applied for, but wasn't successful in any. I had to leave Holy Trinity at the end of June 2007 and by now it was already spring of that year so I was getting very worried. As I was living in a house that went with the job I was facing being left homeless as well as unemployed.

Concerned I wouldn't find a ministry job I thought about leaving full time Christian work and going back to secular work instead. I even considered returning to nursing but in the end the thought of going back to that really didn't appeal at all. Although I loved the contact with patients, my aforementioned inability to multi-task means I find it an incredibly stressful occupation. Anyway, even if I had wanted to return to nursing, my nurse registration was no longer valid. I would need to complete a return to nursing course first. When I phoned for advice about returning to nursing I was told that having been out of it for so long I would not be offered a place on such a course until I had worked as a health care assistant for six to twelve months first. Going back to nursing wasn't the answer.

Then in April, about two months before I was due to leave, a friend from Church Army suggested I advertise myself in the 'looking for work' section on the New Wine[10] leader's network. I hadn't even known there was a job section at all let alone a 'looking for work' section. Suddenly I had hope of finding a way to get a job, so I put up an advert about myself on the site even though it felt like an odd thing to do. Soon afterwards I got a call from Rev Matt Boyes, the then vicar at Christ Church Turnham Green.

Christ Church Turnham Green is a lively Anglican Church in Chiswick, West London only a few miles from Hounslow where I was living. Matt was looking for someone to help Christ Church become more outward looking as a church, to help them fulfill the vision of being 'Church without walls'. I thought that on paper it seemed ideal and as an added bonus it wouldn't seem like such a big relocation if I was only moving a few miles away. Matt and I agreed to meet one Monday morning at Christ Church.

When I arrived at Christ Church I saw a large gothic looking building made of flint with large etched glass

---

10 New Wine is a movement of churches working together to change the nation through a network of church leaders, summer conferences, training events and resources.

He Never Let Go

doors. It was situated in the middle of a green on the south side of Chiswick High Road just in front of the Town Hall. Once I met up with Matt we went over the road to the local Caffè Nero to have a chat about what the post would entail. As we talked over large cups of coffee (meetings held in nearby coffee shops was to become a regular feature of this job) we realized we would work well together and the prospect excited us both. Matt offered me a part time post. I was so relieved. It felt like an enormous weight had been lifted from me. I could breathe easier again.

So, in the September of 2007, I started working part time at Christ Church as their parish evangelist. One of the first things I did was set about training a team of people to keep the church building open every weekday lunchtime. Given its position on Chiswick High Road Christ Church has a lot of people passing the doors but due to a lack of staff these were always locked unless there was a particular event happening.

Three months after I started we opened for our first lunchtime. Not much happened that day but in the months that followed people got to know that the church was open and we had all sorts of people come through the doors. They included amongst others, local workers wanting to pray or meditate in their lunch hour, young mums asking about baptism for their babies, and homeless people looking for a warm seat and a cup of tea.

We had visits from a homeless lady who I had a big soft spot for (she was a regular at Holy Trinity too). She was always so grateful for any food or drink we gave her. She called me 'lady' and loved to sit and tell me all about what had been going on for her. After one lunchtime service that she attended she said,

"Thank you for helping me with my salvation."

That one sentence moved me deeply. I treasure the words she said to me that day.

One part of my job that gave me a lot of joy was the links we made with a local hostel for young single mums. Two of the staff came to a lunchtime carol service we held one year. From that moment on they were regular visitors to our church. As a Church we were able to give Christmas gifts to the girls who were resident in the hostel. One summer we took a few of the young mums and their babies to London Zoo for the day. It was an exhausting day but so worth it. The girls loved it and we enjoyed getting to know them more.

I felt I had more autonomy in my role at Christ Church than I had in previous roles at other churches. I was far more confident about my ministry than I had ever been before. The projects I started were going well, and I felt like a real and proficient parish evangelist for the first time. I had made great friends with people at the church. I knew that I was making a positive impact on the Church as a whole, as well as beginning to make an impact on those outside the church. Also my preaching was really improving and people were responding to my teaching. I'd had a lot of positive comments about how God was using me. So what could possibly go wrong?

8

Lost in broken dreams

"Hope deferred makes the heart sick, but a longing fulfilled is a tree of life." Proverbs 13:12

I never imagined myself as a career girl. I have never had a big career plan because I didn't think I would need one. A career, I thought, wouldn't be the focus of my life. I always thought I would get married, have a home, have children, and be a mum. If I did work outside of the home it wouldn't be the main focus of my life. Any job I had would be to bring in extra money, to get me out of the house. It wouldn't be something to give me a focus for my life. I never dreamed for a moment that I would be single and childless in my late forties, but that is where I found myself. Like many little girls I dreamed of my wedding day. I dreamed of the white dress, the bridesmaids, the flowers, and the handsome groom. I dreamed of a home of my own to look after. I dreamed of children to care for. It really didn't ever occur to me that it might not happen.

I can remember praying quietly to myself in a prayer meeting at All Souls church when I was about twenty or so. I told the Lord that I would go anywhere for Him (and I meant it with all I knew of myself at the time) but I asked Him not to make me go alone. I wonder now if I was putting conditions on God. Maybe deep down I was saying 'I will only go somewhere for you if you give me a husband'. At the time it felt like a plea from my heart, a plea to give me a partner to work with me for Jesus. Only

God knows what was really going on in my heart. To this day, I really don't know. But I do know that that plea has been like a refrain echoing throughout my life, 'Lord, I don't want to be alone'.

One morning when I was at the 1983 Kingdom Faith Christian Camp, a lady prayed for my step-mum, Dinah, who had kidney problems and I joined in with the prayer. At the end of the time of prayer this lady started to pray for me. She prayed that I would have a husband, that I would have a good strong marriage, that we would be equally yoked. I can't remember now the exact words she prayed and I don't remember if she was prophesying or simply asking God for it on my behalf. But I received it as if it were a prophecy, as if it were a statement of what God intended to happen. I was a twenty year old girl dreaming of a husband, a home, and children. I grabbed on to it like a drowning person gasping for air.

Over the years I prayed and I prayed and I prayed for a husband. I prayed on my own. I prayed with others. I prayed and I fasted. I believed that God had spoken to me through the lady at Kingdom Faith camp but also in other ways too. I kept waiting for God to fulfill what I thought was His promise to me. I waited for a husband. I waited but the only weddings I went to were those of other people.

At first, it was fun to see my friends and family get married, thinking that one day I would have a wedding of my own to plan. However, as time went on and more friends got married while I didn't, it got harder and harder to go and keep a smile on my face. It wasn't that I wasn't happy for them because I was delighted. I just wanted it for

He Never Let Go

myself too. I tried to keep my pain to myself, not wanting to ruin anyone's special day.

I began to have questions about whether I would get married. I had questions about whether God always answers our prayers the way we expect. But fear of what the answers might be stopped me consciously acknowledging these questions. I pushed them deep down inside me where I hoped they wouldn't bother me. I did this as usual by overeating the questions away. On the surface I kept telling myself that if I prayed hard enough, if I prayed with enough faith that God would indeed give me a husband.

I had two friends, Elsa and Vivienne, with whom I prayed often about getting married. Elsa and I met at Church and often prayed together about many things, including the desire we both had to get married and have children. We spent many hours in prayer together about it and also about Elsa's need to get British residency (she is originally from the Philippines). I was delighted for Elsa when our prayers about her residency were answered and if I am honest I was pleased for myself too. I wouldn't have wanted to lose my closest friend if she was unable to stay in this country. It gave me hope for my situation too. If God had answered the cry of our hearts for Elsa in this way then surely He would bring us both a husband.

I had met my friend Vivienne at a previous church. We were in the same midweek home Bible study group together. I loved that home group. Sometimes we sang together, with Vivienne's mum playing on the piano. One song we often requested was the beautiful hymn written by

Caroline Maria Noel called 'At the Name of Jesus'. The tune we sang it to is a very stirring tune called Camberwell. It had a particularly rousing bridge between the verses, which lent itself very well for a group of people to join in with it enthusiastically by singing 'dum dum dum'. Consequently it was nicknamed 'The Dum Dum Song'. I'm not sure what newcomers to the group thought when we requested something called The Dum Dum Song, which turned out to be this wonderful classic hymn! They probably thought we were mad and I expect they were right. I still think of that lovely group of people whenever I get the chance to sing 'At the Name of Jesus' to the dum dum tune.

    Whenever Vivienne and I got together outside of home group, we would pray too, maybe not as often as I prayed with Elsa but just as heartfelt. Both Elsa and Vivienne are now married with children and I'm delighted that God answered their prayers. But if I am honest going to their weddings was both a joyful and painful occasion at the same time. There was a huge sense of confusion. Why had God answered our prayers for Elsa and Vivienne but not mine? What had I done wrong? I kept thinking if I just prayed right, or fasted enough, or was good enough, then maybe God would answer my prayers too. I would ask God tearfully,

    "What have I done wrong Lord?"

    Questions like that show what I really believed about God deep down. Asking those questions shows that at a deeper level I was still thinking in terms of a religion of works. I thought I had to earn a husband. I hadn't totally grasped the idea of grace. I thought that if I prayed hard enough, fasted enough, gave to others enough, if I were good enough, God would bless me with a husband. Deep down I believed that the fact that He wasn't blessing me with a husband (and so with children too) meant I hadn't been good enough. But if anyone had asked me if I had to earn blessings from God like that I would have said no, of course not.

My intellect knew that our Father God is a God of grace from whom I don't have to earn a husband. However, my heart still believed in a God who makes you earn everything He gives you. There was obviously a part of me that hadn't grasped the full nature of the gospel of grace. The whole point of Jesus dying on the cross is that we might receive what we do not deserve. There is absolutely no point to Jesus dying if we still have to earn all that we need by performing good works. Good works are our loving, grateful response to the grace we have received. They are not a means to earn things like a spouse from God.

I was talking to someone still on her way to understanding faith a few months ago. We were talking about forgiveness and I was telling her how God forgives us totally for all we do wrong when we confess from our heart what we have done wrong. Jesus' death and resurrection proves to us that God will forgive us. Her response was that it was too easy. My reply was, "Why do you think Christians get so excited about Jesus and call Him Good News! It is that easy to be forgiven."

This doesn't mean it is easy to live a Christian life.

Being forgiven for our sins when we ask is the easy part. Living a life pleasing to God out of gratitude for this free gift of forgiveness and eternal life is the hard part. Why do we so often forget grace and start thinking we have to keep being good or God will not keep loving or forgiving us? We talk about a Gospel of grace but live as if it is a Gospel of salvation by works. We can know God's grace with our intellect but our actions show what we believe deep down in our hearts. I always claimed to believe in a God of grace who gives to me what I don't deserve but my reaction to my on-going singleness showed that a part of me simply hadn't grasped the true nature of God's grace. The apostle Paul had the same problem with the Galatian Christians. His letter to the Galatians, which we find in the New Testament, was a plea that they remember the free gift of grace because they had gone back to trying to earn their salvation again. Paul likened this to being burdened again by a yoke of slavery.

"It is for freedom that Christ has set us free. Stand firm, then, and do not let yourselves be burdened again by a yoke of slavery." Galatians 5:1

I can remember being told an acronym that helps us to remember what grace meant in Christian terms.

God's
Riches
At
Christ's
Expense

G.R.A.C.E. Grace means that we receive the riches of God for free because of what Christ did on the cross at

He Never Let Go

Calvary. We sinned and he died the death we deserve. He chose to die for us, so that our sins could be totally forgiven and be completely wiped out. We sin. Christ suffered. We gain God's riches. That is grace. I think there are a lot of us who struggle to understand the concept of grace. Like my friend we think to ourselves, 'But that is too easy'. We may understand it at an intellectual level but we can't accept it at a deeper, heart level. I wasted many years trying to 'earn' a husband but it was fruitless. I wonder now whether I went into ministry partly to be able to earn a husband, to earn a home and to earn children.

Although I was successful in my ministry at Christ Church and I enjoyed the actual work, it wasn't satisfying the deep painful longing in my heart for companionship. I realize now that this is one reason why a part of me struggled with the work of parish evangelist a lot of the time. Being an evangelist is not something you should do for misplaced ulterior motives unless you want to drive yourself nearly insane and unfortunately, I can tell you this from bitter experience. What I really wanted was to find a husband, to be a wife, to have my own home, and to have children. I wanted to please God enough so that He would give me those things. Although I did want to serve God from honorable motives as well, deep down part of my motivation was wrong.

I now think my loss of faith was due, to a large extent, to my pushing down and burying this pain of unwanted singleness and childlessness. I let out some pain but not all of it. Some of it I was eating down as I continued in my self-destructive eating patterns, trying but failing to control the pain by overeating. All I did was get more overweight and I stayed desperately sad. Grief at my situation filled me but I only took to God the overflow of what I felt. It was as if I was a container full of pain. I didn't take it to God until the pain was overflowing the container. Then I only let out enough to stop the overflow. The rest of the deep pain festered inside and ate away at me and at my belief in God, while I binged on any sweet food I could lay my hands on to try to anaesthetize what I wasn't letting out to God. I reacted to the pain by beginning to question God but I just ignored the doubts and the deep pain. I pushed it all down deep inside, telling myself I had to be a good Christian and let the desire for marriage go. This was happening over many years of my life. It has been a constant undercurrent to all else that was going on around me. I never wanted to be single and the pain was eating away at me.

If only I had taken King David's advice years ago I might have spared myself some of the pain I have felt. In psalm 62:7-8 he wrote the following words.

"My salvation and my honor depend on God;
he is my mighty rock, my refuge.
Trust in him at all times, O people;
pour out your hearts to him,
for God is our refuge."

Pour your hearts out to the Lord. Really pour them out. Don't do as I did and just tip a little of the overflow to Him. Pour it all out to Him.

He Never Let Go

Unwanted singleness got harder the older I became. When I was in my twenties I was still concentrating on other things such as getting settled into a career. I had a lot of close single friends. While I was younger getting married and having children was still a realistic dream. It got harder when I got older. When I could no longer say I was in my early thirties it started to get much worse. Suddenly it seemed as if time was running out. The sands were running rapidly through the hourglass of time and there was nothing I could do to stop them.

With women in particular the biological clock starts to tick very loudly. I knew that if I wasn't married and seriously trying to have a baby by the time I was forty then my chances of ever being a mother were diminished so greatly that they were nearly impossible. If like me you have always wanted to have a family, it is an incredibly hard time. By the time I was in my late thirties/early forties most of my contemporaries already had spouses and children, and panic started to set in. When I was that age I felt more left out, alone and sad than I can ever begin to make you understand if you have not experienced it. The pain is excruciating.

Unfortunately, the wider church isn't always a place of refuge for us singles, particularly those of us who are older and still want to get married, or who are grieving not having had children. It sometimes feels like the church doesn't know what to do with us. They don't know quite how to deal with our pain. They love us but they don't necessarily understand us. Many church leaders in the protestant church are married and have families. Many have been married since their mid twenties, so they have simply not had the experience of unwanted on-going singleness. It's an alien experience and it can be very hard for them to know how to help us. They want to help us but their life experience makes it hard for them to know where to start. I don't envy them their task. So many of them are simply not equipped for what is before them when dealing with us.

Many churches I have belonged to want to create a family atmosphere, which is great. However, this often ends up meaning a church service where children are accepted. I think it is vital that families with young children are welcomed in church and can enjoy a service without being worried about how people will react to their child. It is very important that we continue to welcome families like that and I love it when children are involved in a service. But I think we also need to remember the other people in a family. We need to remember the older people and the singles, as well as many others I haven't mentioned. I have come across some churches which do put on activities for single people, but it is often called the 20-30's group. When you are single and in your forties that almost feels like a statement that you have failed if you are over thirty nine, still single and wish you weren't.

Some Churches put on courses and events to give help to those who are married and parents such as the marriage course, marriage preparation and parenting classes. I hope more churches will have the skills and facilities to put on events like these. They are so necessary and can help bring God's healing, truth and love to those who need it. But where is the help for single people to be single? There seems to be an assumption by some people that because we all start out single it is easy to be single and therefore it shouldn't be a problem. If we do find it a problem then we are left wondering sometimes if there is something wrong with us. We are sometimes left feeling that our relationship with God is lacking or that if we were better Christians we would be happy as single people.

Over the years I have sometimes shared with other Christians my feelings about singleness and childlessness and asked for prayer. Rather than helping doing this has often left me feeling a failure and a bad example of a Christian. Some people would say I should pray hard and God will give me a husband. It's what you might call the 'name it and claim it' attitude. I always have to work really hard not to be sarcastic about it if people say that to me. I am always so tempted to say sarcastically 'Pray about it – gosh as a Christian who prays about most things in my life that had never occurred to me. Thanks for the advice. I will start praying now'.

The truth is that I've been praying about it for about twenty five years. It is not as simple as just asking God for a spouse and He will give you one. For various reasons it doesn't always work like that. We don't always get what we want in life. I don't have enough room in this book[11] to explore why prayer appears to go unanswered sometimes but for now I will say this. Prayer isn't like a vending

---

[11] I can recommend a book about this subject called God on Mute by Pete Greig ISBN-10: 1842913174

machine. I can't simply put in enough prayer and God produces what I want. All of us have things in life that are hard for us to cope with and that we would like God to take away. I wish God had taken away my singleness and had given me the joy of having children but He didn't. However, I am in good company when it comes to unanswered prayers. St Paul asked for his thorn in the flesh to be removed three times but it wasn't. Instead God said to him each time he asked for it to be removed,

"My grace is sufficient for you, for my power is made perfect in weakness" (2 Corinthians 12:9).

The other way people reacted was to tell me that I must be making an idol out of marriage and God would not answer my prayers until I stop idolizing it. They told me I had to 'lay marriage down', or to 'sacrifice it', which implied to me that wanting marriage was a sin or something that wasn't to be encouraged. It also felt like I was being told that I was not a good example of a Christian if I still wanted to get married one day. After all I had God in my life, they seemed to say, you shouldn't still want marriage. Things like that made me angry and hurt rather than helped me a lot of the time. It was almost like being told that my motives had to be pure before God would allow me to be married. Personally, I don't think any of us has totally pure motives for anything we do. This line of argument was subtly reinforcing my subconscious view of Christianity being a religion of works again. I had to earn a husband by how I thought or what I did.

I don't think it is as simple as having the wrong

motives, or not praying enough. Maybe there are no answers. Bad things happen. Some married people wish they were still single and some single people wish they were married. Sometimes married people experience childlessness despite years of praying for a child. No-one's life is plain sailing. Jesus never promised us we would have an easy life. Life is often hard for all of us no matter what our marital state. We have to learn to deal with the hardships with God's help and with that of our fellow Christians as well as celebrating each other's joys too.

I didn't often ask people to help me pray about my unhappiness with singleness after receiving answers like the ones above. Not only did it not help but also it made me feel worse. I realize that the people giving me these answers wanted to be helpful and had the best of intentions for me. It is simply unfortunate that they were unable to help me in the way they hoped. I think I just needed to be able to express my pain and have someone help me find Jesus despite the pain or even within the pain.

I have spent years of my life feeling really guilty for wanting to get married one day. I picked up the idea that I am a poor example of a Christian if God is not enough for me. I have wasted years trying not to want marriage because I thought I was being sinful and unfaithful to God by wanting it. Actually God knows we need companionship with other humans as well as fellowship with Him. I think it is important to note that God created Eve for Adam. He didn't create a platonic best friend or provide a home group, he created Adam a wife. This doesn't mean a spouse is the only cure for loneliness by a long way but it does mean that wanting one is not sinful or wrong. It is a normal part of being human.

Simply wanting marriage doesn't mean I will get married. I need to move to a place of acceptance with my life as it is. But if I am to get to that place I need to start from the premise that I am normal for wanting marriage just as it is also normal not to want it. I need to start from the base line that the suffering of unwanted singleness is a justified suffering. Starting from this position gives me a firm place from which I can really move forward. I can grieve for my loss and then I can give my pain to God and ask Him to use it for His glory. While I thought the desire for marriage was a sin I felt unable to give it to God in that way. A sin is something to be confessed. A sin isn't something in which I ask God to glorify Himself. While I had the idea that wanting marriage was some kind of sin I was stuck in neutral gear, unable to move forward at all. I was trapped in suppressed pain. Seeing my pain as normal and justified has been absolutely vital in enabling me to deal with the situation in which I find myself.

It is normal to want marriage and it is normal not to want marriage. I want to be clear that I don't think that being married is any easier than being single, just as being single isn't any easier than being married. I believe that marriage and singleness are differently difficult. They are such different states of being that it is hard to compare them. However, if we find ourselves wanting marriage but remaining single it produces suffering. When some of us struggle with singleness there are not many places we can go where we are understood. Some people love being single and it is not a hardship for them. But there are some of us who are not designed to be long term singles. I am one of those people. I find living alone hard. It is part of my nature I guess.

We can all expect to suffer at times but that suffering can be made worse when people who should be supporting you don't see your suffering as suffering. When our suffering is seen as a character or spiritual flaw it adds to our pain rather than helps with it. That applies to all types of suffering not just unwanted singleness. I think help with our various sufferings starts with someone coming alongside us, identifying to a certain extent with our pain and enabling us to express it. It helps us move onwards to change or acceptance.

A more helpful response would be along the lines of this. 'It is quite normal for you to feel this pain. There is nothing wrong with you and you have not failed God. How can I help you to express your pain so that you can begin to move forward into a life of fulfillment whether that is marriage or accepting singleness?'

My prayer is that over time more support will be given to church leaders/churches/single people to help singles work towards a life of fulfillment within their singleness.

I now know that wanting the companionship of marriage is not wrong for a Christian. I've come to see that it's a normal biological urge. It's natural for living beings to want to mate and reproduce. I also accept that it doesn't mean that God will automatically produce a mate out of thin air. It does mean that I am now starting from a place of acceptance of that desire. I no longer view having that desire as a sign of being a 'bad' Christian. I am not letting God down by feeling as I do. It gives me a much firmer base from which to continue my search for wholeness. Starting from the premise that the desire was wrong in itself gave me a false foundation and I could never quite move on from it. Now that I am starting from a place of reality I know for sure that I can move on to find fulfillment in life whether that is as a single or married person. It has been a long journey and I hope that I can help others so they don't have to go through what I have. However, when I was working at Christ Church Turnham Green I hadn't dealt with the pain at all. I was still hiding it all inside.

Chiswick was a lovely place to live and I liked the atmosphere of the area. My work was going well; I was succeeding at my job. I expect other people looking at my life saw how well things were going and thought that everything was good for me. They didn't know how desperately I was struggling with the pain of unwanted singleness and therefore childlessness. I was drowning in it. Slowly and gradually, I was being pulled under by an incredibly deep pain that I had pushed down inside me. I don't think I had any idea how much pressure was building up inside me until it all came to a head one Sunday after church. It was sometime in late summer or early autumn 2009, I think.

Christ Church Turnham Green is filled with delightful, loving and kind people. One lady in particular was very

He Never Let Go

loving and understanding to me. One Sunday after the service, she asked me how I was. She knew I was struggling but I don't think she had any idea what would happen when she asked that one simple question, 'how are you'. All of a sudden all the pain and anguish I had felt for so many years came up and I knew it needed to be let out. I was horrified when I realized I couldn't keep my tears at bay. It was an awful moment when all the tears came so far up that nothing could stop them anymore. The dam burst. We were in the coffee area at the time with lots of people milling about us. I put my hand over my mouth hoping I could keep the tears in, 'I can't cry here!' I thought. My friend saw what was happening to me and led me gently back into the church worship area and sat me down on a seat. What took place in the next few minutes was simultaneously some of the most painful and the most beautiful, moments of my life.

As soon as I sat down my companion put her arm around my shoulders. I felt all the pain and anguish come tumbling out in torrents of sobbing and stuttering words. A tidal wave of deep pain had started to come gushing up inside me and I simply couldn't hold it in. I thought that I was going to be swallowed up in all that agony. I felt I was drowning in it all. This angel of mercy simply sat there, held my hand, and said,

"Just let it out, I am here with you and Jesus is here with you. You aren't alone."

There was no judging, no trying to make me stop crying. There were no trite words or phrases. There was just unconditional love and acceptance of my pain. This amazing, beautiful, and Godly woman was simply there with me in my anguish. That's what made it so beautiful even though it was so painful. That's what makes it one of those moments I shall never forget. From what she says now my friend may not have been feeling as Christ-like in that situation as I felt her to be. I think that is so amazing of God. We give Him what we can in faith and He takes our efforts and makes them so much more by His Spirit. This lady was used greatly by God that day no matter what was going on in her! Being allowed to let the pain out in God's presence was life changing even if it has taken a long while to deal with the aftermath.

9

Doubt settles in

At first, I felt better for having let out all that pain but things changed over the next few weeks. I just couldn't believe that God, who was supposed to love me, would allow me to feel all that pain and disappointment. I was feeling hollowed out, empty, but at the same time, I started feeling angry with Him. All the anger I had held back with the pain was coming out too. 'Why God' seemed to echo round my mind all the time.

"I thought you loved me Lord" I cried to Him

Of course, I now know that God wasn't in control of how I dealt with my pain. I have free will and that is down to me. He longed that I would pour it all out to Him. He longed to be able to help me with what was going on but I had been keeping Him out of it. But if I thought letting out and dealing (or not as the case may be) with all that pain was distressing enough, I was in for even worse sorrow when I found myself in the darkest months I have ever been through.

It happened slowly and gradually. Little by little, over the course of that autumn I became aware of a gradual erosion of my faith in the existence of God. I keep a journal and in it I sometimes write down the prayers I pray. At first, after I spent that time sobbing on someone's shoulder, I started writing 'If you are there Lord'. To be honest I have had times before when I was going through a bad time that I would write 'If you are there Lord'. The previous times it was just a few hours at a time I felt like that, and then only once in a while. I think that is normal. But this time, unlike before, it didn't stop. Over the weeks, 'If you are there Lord . . .' starting turning into 'There is no God'. It's as if the unbelief tiptoed so slowly into my mind that I didn't really notice it.

I remember a game we used to play as children. It was called Grandma's footsteps. One child stood at one end of the room facing the wall. This child was 'Grandma' (no matter what sex the child was they were called 'Grandma'). The rest of us were at the other end of the room, and we had to creep slowly and quietly towards 'Grandma' whose back was still turned to us. Those creeping up had to try to get near enough to 'Grandma' to touch her without being seen to move. 'Grandma' could turn around briefly any time she liked. If she saw you move, she would point to you and you had to go back to the start. If she didn't see you move you could stay where you were. The aim was to make it all the way up to 'Grandma' and tap her on the shoulder without her knowing you were there. I felt as if my doubts had been creeping up stealthily behind me like the children in that game. When I turned around they didn't seem to be moving, but all of a sudden, they had reached up and grabbed hold of me.

I don't suppose I am the only one who has had things creep up on her. How often do we allow things to sneak into our lives? Unhelpful attitudes, thoughts, and actions become a part of our consciousness slowly but surely, until suddenly, we realize how much we have changed. At first, I thought my loss of faith was just a short phase I was going through. I believed that I would 'snap out of it' relatively quickly. I thought it was just a longer version of the brief moments of doubt I had had before and I would go back to believing in the existence of God again within a few weeks. I was wrong. In all it lasted more than a year.

I remember feeling a deep sense of shame and guilt about my loss of faith. I was an evangelist. I was supposed to be telling others how wonderful God was in sending us His Son to die for our sins. I was supposed to be telling people about the amazing love and forgiveness of God through Jesus. This wasn't how it was meant to be. When I stood in front of the Archbishop of York in Sheffield cathedral to be admitted into the office of evangelist in July 2003 this wasn't in my 10-year plan!

With the benefit of hindsight I now think I was in shock as well. Until that point, my belief in the existence of God had always been so deep-seated. I couldn't accept that my belief in God had simply vanished like a puff of smoke. Like a cloud being blown away by the wind, it had just gone. It seemed so unreal. I felt like I was walking around in a dream. No, not a dream, it was like being in a nightmare, an awful never ending nightmare. 'I'll wake up in a minute,' I would think. I really wanted to wake up and have everything go back to what it was beforehand. It didn't.

Once I realized that my faith in God had indeed evaporated I started to panic, which added to the stress I was feeling. Working as a parish evangelist meant my whole life was connected to my faith. My job, my home, and most of my social life were all dependant on my faith in God. My job was sharing my faith in God, using words and action, to the people living and working in Chiswick. Sharing the action of my faith wasn't a problem. I still cared a lot about the people of Chiswick. But sharing my faith in words was much, much harder. Having found myself with no faith, I had to start sharing what I thought was a lie to the people around me. This was so very stressful for me. I hated speaking and living a lie. I felt like I was being dishonest with people. I have too much integrity to be able to keep on telling people something I thought was untrue. But at the same time, I was terrified of being forced to leave and start all over again. My dislike of being dishonest about my faith wasn't as bad as the thought of leaving and starting over again. I didn't know what I would do if I wasn't in parish ministry. It was just like the situation I faced when I started to think about leaving ministry at the end of my first post. As before, I knew nursing again wasn't the answer. So, not knowing what else to do I kept on ignoring the doubts and hoped faith would just come back one day.

The longer this battle with myself went on, the more afraid I became at losing my job. For me it wasn't just losing a job and a career that worried me. I lived in a apartment that went with the job. Leaving the job would mean having nowhere to live. The thought of being possibly homeless was really difficult to deal with. It was harder than the thought of being unemployed. My constant dream of a home of my own was unraveling. I did know however that I would always have a roof over my head. I have too many good friends and family who wouldn't have seen me living on the streets. But over the years I have learned from experience that there is a big difference between having a roof over your head and having a home. I have never been without a roof over my head, and I doubt I ever will but sometimes I have lived in places that didn't feel like home. Now, with the loss of my faith, I was facing the fact that I would have to move house once again. I have moved so often in my adult life and I feel more upset by each move. I dreaded having to try to settle into yet another place. A settled home was such a deep-rooted longing that I couldn't face the idea of moving once more.

Most of my social life was tied up around church too. The nature of the work means committing regularly to social events outside of church is very hard, although I did have one thing which I managed to get to. I found a book group that met at 5pm at Chiswick Business Park. It was great. I met people unconnected with Church and talked about things that generally didn't have anything to do with God. It was a big blessing. Apart from that group, virtually everything else about my life in Chiswick was associated with my faith in God. Losing my faith was bad enough but the thought that I could lose my job, home and social life as well made it all seem so much worse.

I know now I should have confided in a Christian I trusted about how my faith had disappeared. However, fear of rejection, and a fear of having to leave my job sooner than I was ready to, meant I hid what I was thinking. I didn't talk about it to anyone. Instead all I did was binge eat to try to bury the feelings that were overwhelming me.

It crossed my mind fleetingly to speak about my problems to my vicar, Matt. Matt is one of the least judgmental people I have ever known. He is very loving and gentle. Had I been an ordinary member of the congregation I wouldn't have hesitated telling him. I know his reaction would have been as loving and gentle as if Jesus himself were sitting in front of me. What prevented me telling him was the fact that he was employing me to share my faith, a faith I no longer had. He had employed me as an evangelist. I didn't want to put him in an awkward position with the rest of the church leadership team so I said nothing. Fear had sunk its icy fingers into the depths of my being. I was too scared of unemployment and homelessness to tell anyone what was happening to me. It made it an incredibly lonely time.

Everything in my life was upside down. My long held dreams of being a wife and a mother were in tatters around my feet, leaving me feeling empty and not knowing which way to look for fulfillment. As usual I sought that fulfillment in overeating, trying to fill the emptiness with food but it still didn't fill the gap for more than a few hours. With the evaporation of my faith in God the career I thought I had discovered later in my life was also disappearing. It was a time of conflicting emotions. Although this was a time of being too scared to leave my job, I badly wanted to. Every conversation I had about God with a parishioner and every Bible study I had to lead tore

He Never Let Go

me up. I was saying one thing and believing another. Everything was in turmoil and I didn't know how to cope with it all. It was a time of not knowing what was happening to me. It was a time of great darkness, and eerie shadows. I had no God to lean on and I hadn't told anyone about what was happening. I felt very isolated and alone. Food was my only friend.

Having said that, in the end I did tell one person. I told my sister Caroline. She had been through a similar thing to me and is now an atheist. She listened to me with immense kindness and understanding. I knew she would. That is why I told her. Firstly, she is naturally kind, understanding, and thoughtful. Secondly, she had become an atheist and had experienced changing one's beliefs first hand.

However, I was fearful of telling Christians. I guess I thought I would be rejected, or worse given a long lecture about how there was a God. I knew neither response would help me believe in God again. In fact I was fairly sure both of those things would send me further away from coming back to a belief in God.

Life for me then was like the going down of the sun. The light got gradually weaker and the darkness got gradually stronger. I didn't realize how dark it had become until the carol service that year. The panic I felt when Matt asked me to preach was a huge clue to how far from God I had come but it was the carol service itself that really made me aware of my total lack of belief in God. It was like that moment when you suddenly realize it's got dark outside and you haven't realized until then. You look up and there is just darkness where there was once light. It was like that for me that Christmas. I looked up and suddenly there was darkness where there had previously been the light of Christ.

That evening in December 2009 after the 'Carols by Candlelight' service, as I walked back to my car to drive home, I was sure of one fact. I had to get really serious about finding another job and a home. My sanity depended on it. I determined to get up the next day and start an earnest search for another career.

Earlier in the year I had bought a book called 'What color is your parachute' by Richard Bolles. At the time I bought it I was only half heartedly thinking of leaving the job and the book had been sitting unread on the bookshelf for weeks. My reaction to having to preach at the carol service now gave me the impetus I needed to read it. The next morning I got it off the shelf and read it, making notes as I went. I found it very helpful indeed.

There is a series of very useful exercises in this book, which got me thinking about what skills I have that could be transferred to another career. Other questions got me thinking about things such as, what part of the country I wanted to live in and how much money I needed to earn. I knew I still wanted to work with people. If I don't have a job where I can regularly talk to people, it drives me insane. I need to be paid to talk to people! In addition, I knew I wanted to be near people I already knew well. I didn't want to move to an area where I knew no one. I decided I would look for a job in two places. Firstly, I

He Never Let Go

looked in Sussex where I grew up and where my mum Patricia, and step-dad Patrick live. Secondly, I looked on the East London and Essex border near Woodford where I used to live, and where my best friend Elsa and her family live.

After a time of thinking about it, I realized my skills would suit, and I would probably enjoy, being a warden in a block of sheltered housing. It would also provide accommodation into the bargain. So, I set about looking for a job as a warden of sheltered housing in those two areas of Sussex or Woodford. I researched the companies in England that provide sheltered housing and then regularly looked at each company's website for jobs.

However, in the meantime I still had to get on with working as a parish evangelist despite no longer believing in the existence of God. Sometimes the strain of living a lie was so great that I tried to convince myself I really did believe in Him. I wanted things to go back to what they were like before. But they didn't. I had to keep running Bible studies; I had to keep encouraging people to believe things that I no longer thought were true. When leading LunchBytes, our lunch time Bible study, I tried to make sure I didn't have to say anything about what I thought. I would try to get people interacting with the Bible themselves, giving as little input as I could. I found that this actually helped people get more out of the study because they tended to really grapple with the parts of the text that caught their eye. I also liked it when there were a lot of people at the study because the conversation was carried more easily without me saying anything. I am amazed now that no-one saw through my little tricks!

At the beginning of 2010 two of us from church set up Sunbeams baby and toddler group. It was very successful and we had a lot of mums (and nannies, grandmas, dads and aunties) coming into the church, most of whom didn't regularly attend church. It was a part of my role I could cope with better than others because I didn't have to talk about my faith, or lack of it at all. My colleague had a baby and so she was the person who mixed with the mums. I was the one at the door who welcomed people and who made tea and coffee for everyone. It was hard work but I enjoyed it. I didn't have to lie about who I was. I love meeting new people and I love babies. Sunbeams gave me plenty of both! It helped me make it through the six months before I actually left.

Sundays were hard work. I had to sit through worship services that I didn't want to be at. I had to go through the motions of singing and praying. It was very hard. Sometimes I put on such a good act I almost believed it myself. At times I think I was trying to convince myself that I still believed so I could stay where I was and avoid the upheaval.

The friend on whose shoulder I had sobbed so hard was still praying with me sometimes and I didn't tell her the whole story about how much I had stopped believing. I hoped that the prayer with her would cure my doubts. But it didn't. With hindsight, without her knowing the full story, she was unable to pray effectively for me. The prayer sessions made me feel good because someone was caring about me and giving me attention. When answering the question 'What is God saying to you?' I answered automatically saying whatever came into my mind. At the time, I didn't think I was really hearing God. I thought my sub-conscious was trying to find God where he used to be. Looking back now I think God was trying to speak to me and I may even have heard him, but I simply didn't take it on board.

I never did tell Matt about my loss of faith while I was still working at Christ Church. I told him after I had left. He was so kind about it. His reaction made me realize he would have been very gentle and would have helped all he could. I wish I had trusted him more and told him what was going on because it would have made a hard time that little bit easier.

I sent in a few applications for posts as a sheltered housing warden but I wasn't short listed for any of them. Then after a few months, as I looked over my previous applications a light bulb went on in my head. It occurred to me that having my two previous job titles as 'Parish Evangelist' might not be helpful when applying to non-Christian organizations. The word evangelist can have many negative associations for people who are not used to it. It is often associated with weird TV evangelists who demand money from people in the name of the Lord. Even if that is not the image there is a sub-conscious concern that we will go around bashing people over the head with a big thick leather Bible. So, with Matt's permission, I decided to change my job title to 'Community Worker' instead. It described my role accurately so I didn't feel I was being underhand. My brief when starting the job had been to get the Church and the community interacting with each other more.

A little while after changing the name of my job title I saw an advert on a website for a post as a residential manager at a small block of retirement apartments in Peacehaven, East Sussex. It sounded right up my street. Peacehaven is on the south east coast of England, situated on the Greenwich Meridian. The town lies on top of the cliffs a few miles east of Brighton. My mum and step-dad live in Lewes, which is about seven miles from Peacehaven so it seemed an ideal job to go for. I applied for the post. Perhaps the change of job title worked because I was delighted when I was offered an interview. Maybe I would have been given the interview anyway I don't know. But this interview seemed to be the lifeline I was looking for.

The day of my interview was a bright, sunny, and warm June day. Staying with my parents the night before the interview meant I was able to arrive nice and early in Peacehaven. I had time to sit on the cliff top a few hundred yards from the block of apartments where the interview was taking place and look at the sea to prepare myself. It was a lovely, calm day with a blue sky above the sea, which shone and glistened in the sunlight. I relished the smell of the salty sea water as a gentle breeze blew in my face. It was glorious. I suddenly knew that this was the place I wanted to be. I walked up to the interview with renewed enthusiasm for the job.

As I arrived at the block of 1980's red brick apartments I was met by a professional looking, attractive woman with long fair hair and a warm smile. I liked her immediately. I felt relaxed during the interview, which was held in the apartment that I would occupy should I get the job. I was confident when I walked away that I had done as good a job as I could at convincing the interviewers that I would be right for the job.

Some days later, while attending a meeting in Church, I got a call from my prospective employer. I left the meeting and standing outside the church building in the dusk, my new boss offered me the job.

I was absolutely delighted and accepted straight away. I only needed to give a month's notice and was due to start at my new job in Peacehaven in just four weeks time. I had a lot to organize in a short space of time. I decided to treat myself to having the removal men pack for me. I had packed myself the last time I moved and it was totally exhausting. It was so worth the extra money paying someone else to do it for me. I arrived at my new home at 3pm on Friday 16th July. I had just one weekend to unpack before starting my job on Monday 19th. I was so tired when the removal men left I could barely move. I had virtually no food, no cooker, and no fridge so I walked to the nearby carvery for a meal. I was shattered. Each step felt tougher to make than the one before it. My legs were made of lead by now I was sure. It must have taken about 20 minutes for me to walk slowly and painfully to the restaurant. The walk is actually only ten minutes so I must have been very tired that day.

Although it left me physically done in, I knew as soon as I moved into my new place that I had done the right thing. I was free from the lie I had been living. It was as if a massive weight had been lifted from my shoulders. I was almost bemused by the freedom I felt. I thought that when I moved away from London and from church ministry I had moved away from God. I thought this was the start of my life as a dedicated atheist. How little I knew!

10

Adjusting

Now, after thirteen years of working in full time Christian work in some way or another, I had left ministry and was once more in a 'normal' job. I thought that this was the beginning of the rest of my life. A week after starting my job I left to go on a holiday that I had booked months previously while still working at Christ Church Turnham Green. I was going to New Wine, a Christian camp held in Somerset in the south west of England. I was booked in with a group from Christ Church and this year unlike other years I had booked a caravan rather than being under canvas. I was tempted not to go because it is Christian and I didn't want any spiritual input. However, the caravan rental hadn't been cheap so I decided to go but not attend any of the meetings. I would see it as a restful holiday with friends. I was sure that my Christ Church friends would see how absent my belief in God was but if they did they didn't say. In order to explain my absence at meetings I told them I was exhausted from the move and just wanted to rest. They seemed to believe me and I managed to have a really restful holiday. It did feel strange to be at New Wine but not go to meetings.

I did try to pray while I was at New Wine. It seemed appropriate while spending a week at this Christian camp even though I didn't think God was there any more. I had a small sketch pad with me and one day I sat drawing whatever came to me without much conscious thought about my actions. I began by drawing myself sitting in the hand of God and included the words 'What I'm feeling, or thinking doesn't change the fact that I'm in God's hand'.

'Psalm 91' was also written next to my sketch to remind me of this lovely Psalm which speaks of God's protection. Verse 4 of Psalm 91 reminds me of the words I wrote. It says,

"He will cover you with his feathers, and under his wings you will find refuge".

Another similar sketch had the words 'Sometimes its dark because I'm protecting you, my hands are wrapped around you'.

I barely remember drawing and writing these things now. I think I kidded myself that it was my subconscious mind putting down what I thought God would have said to me before I stopped believing in Him. I put what I had drawn and written out of my mind almost as soon as I had put my pencil down. Now I am amazed as I pick up that sketch book that God still spoke to me despite my no longer believing in Him. That is grace. That is love. God was with me, and speaking to me, even though I didn't have faith that He even existed. I had turned my back on Him but still he spoke tenderly to me. It reminds me of a verse from the Old Testament book of Hosea. It is God speaking to Israel as if she were an unfaithful wife.

"Therefore I am now going to allure her; I will lead her into the desert and speak tenderly to her." (Hosea 2:14)

He Never Let Go

When I got back to work I still couldn't work out what had happened to me or why it had happened but I believed I was now free. I realize now that I was in a honeymoon period when the freedom from the demands of ministry was almost intoxicating to me. I found myself working Monday to Friday 9am to 5pm for the first time in ages. I hadn't had sociable working hours for so long that it seemed a real treat to have evenings and weekends off. If I wanted to go away for a weekend I could do so without asking for permission from my boss. It almost felt like being on holiday all the time. Luxury!

I made the most of my new found freedom and I joined various activities going on in my area. I became a member of two local, but very different book clubs and the local group of the National Women's Register[12]. In all my years of working in churches I had never had so many friends outside the church, or so much time to go and follow my own interests. I was reveling in it. I felt like a kid let loose in a sweet shop. It's ironic that I didn't really get to know this many non-Christians until after I stopped being a paid evangelist.

I did keep going to church sometimes when I moved. I wasn't yet ready to change the habit of a lifetime. After all, I had been a Christian for twenty eight years by the time I moved to Sussex and for most of those years I had gone to church on a Sunday. I was, however, delighted that I didn't have to go if I didn't want to. I could stay in bed on Sunday

---

12 National Women's register 'is a network of local groups and individual members who enjoy lively discussion and conversation, both serious and light-hearted'

morning. Sometimes annoyingly, I did still feel guilty about missing church. But I thought it was just a matter of time before I let go of all the old Christian attitudes. I was convinced by now that I was becoming an atheist, that I was de-converting. I was just building up the courage needed to make the final split with church and religion, and so make a new life for myself. I believed I had out grown and was leaving behind the myth of God.

Once I acknowledged to myself that I no longer believed in the existence of God, I thought that was it. The religious part of my life had come to an end. I had arrived. I had finally grown up. I was now an atheist. All I had to do now was simply learn to live as a non-Christian. This in itself felt like a challenge. After all, I had become a Christian as a young eighteen year old and all my adult life, up to that point, had been lived as a committed Christian. I'd always had the Church and my faith to help me know how to live. I had now lost my life-long frame of reference for living and would have to find a new one. I thought it would be an atheist one but I would need to find a new reason for the existence of the universe, which didn't include God.

I remember reading Richard Dawkins' book, 'The God Delusion' while I still had my faith. Contrary to what Professor Dawkins was hoping, the first time I read it some of his arguments convinced me even more that there is a God rather than convincing me that there isn't. Now I was thinking again about some of the things that I had read previously in Professor Dawkins' book. He seems so convinced by reason and scientific thinking that there is no

He Never Let Go

God. Now I was beginning to agree with him. This was a big shock to me, having at first reacted to his beliefs by being more assured of the truth of Christianity.

I may have misunderstood his arguments when I first read them. From what I understood, he seemed to be saying the universe is complex and improbable and therefore, God is complex and improbable. I agreed with the part about the universe being complex but the rest of his argument didn't make as much sense to me. God may be complex but the idea of God being improbable because the universe is improbable seemed to me even more illogical. If it is improbable that something could come into existence on its own without outside help surely that means outside help is more likely not less likely? When I first read 'The God delusion' the belief Professor Dawkins describes defied any logic I had. The whole idea of the universe being complicated and improbable made it seem more likely to me that there is a Creator God behind it, not less likely. Back then I just couldn't make the leap to there being no God. In fact it was at that moment in reading Professor Dawkins' book that I had what one might call an epiphany. I just knew beyond all doubt that there is a God.

But now, although I still didn't agree with all Professor Dawkins was saying, I was stunned to realize I was beginning to agree with him about there being no God. His descriptions of how the world began were making more sense and I was beginning to see the possibility of the universe coming into existence without God. I never thought for a moment that was remotely possible. Atheism seemed to be settling into my mind.

11

Newton's Cradle

Well, my 'learning to live as an atheist' plan didn't quite work out as I planned. The honeymoon period of living without God was over and reality was setting in. What actually happened was that rather than settling happily into an atheist lifestyle as I imagined, I began to feel like a Newton's Cradle. My thoughts started swinging wildly from one extreme to another.

I can remember being fascinated as a teenager with a Newton's Cradle the first time I saw one. For those who haven't seen one Newton's Cradle is a series of five steel balls hanging in a line from wires on a metal frame. When you swing one ball against the other four, the ball at the other end of the line starts to swing. When it swings back it also hits the four balls and makes the original ball start to swing again, and so it goes on. I couldn't drag my eyes away from the steel balls as they swung back and forth. There has been an advert for Kit Kat chocolate bars on British TV recently set on a building site. During the site work break (when as the advert implies one should be eating a Kit Kat) a group of five workmen operating cranes with wrecking balls gradually get into line to form a giant Newton's Cradle. The advert ends with the balls starting to swing against one another. I would love to have a go at that one day! Anyway I'm now rambling.

He Never Let Go

That image of a giant Newton's Cradle described my thoughts about God completely. They were fluctuating hugely. One moment I thought my faith in God was returning and things would go back to normal again. The next moment I was back to thinking 'there is no God'. I didn't know what I was thinking. It was all a mass of confusion. I just hoped that the swinging would stop in due course, like a Newton's Cradle stops eventually. I got very impatient wanting it to stop right away. The constant movement back and forth was making me nauseous. I wanted to know what I believed but I simply couldn't work it out.

It felt foolish not knowing what I believed about God's existence because I had previously been so convinced about it. Before my crisis of faith, I couldn't see how anyone could fail to see that there is a Creator God behind our universe. It had all seemed so obvious to me that He was there. The universe is so amazing and intricate that I couldn't see how it could happen by chance. For me the biggest proof of God's existence is life itself. I couldn't see how life had started without God. Even if life started out as an amoeba and evolved into what it is today, something had to make it live. Life, I reasoned to myself, could not just start from nowhere. Over the last year that had changed. Now, for most of the time, I couldn't believe there is a God. I couldn't understand how life had started from nothing but I accepted it must have done if there is no God. The change in my beliefs was such a strange feeling that it felt like walking around in shoes that are the wrong size and shape for my feet.

The certainty of my faith in God had gone already. But now the newfound certainty that there is no God also disappeared for some of the time. Although mostly, I simply couldn't believe in God and it seemed ridiculous to think He was there, in a twinkling of an eye that assurance in God's non-existence would disappear. I would see the sun sinking into the sea at the end of my road, throwing stunning orange and golden light over the English Channel and my thoughts swung again. I would look at that beautiful sunset and the inner voice I had always thought was God, started to speak to me about a Creator God. It was as if the sky itself was crying out 'There is a God'. As the Psalmist says in Psalm 19:1,

"The heavens declare the glory of God; the skies proclaim the work of his hands"

And so there on a cliff top watching the sun sink into the sea, the steel balls of my beliefs swung back the other way again. But immediately I would counteract it and I would talk myself out of hearing that voice as God. I would say to myself 'that is the inner voice that I used to think was God but now I know it isn't'. And so the steel balls of belief once more swung the other way.

A part of me wanted someone to tell me what to believe. I wanted someone to say, 'This is what is happening to you and this is what you must believe, and this is what you should do to get right with God again'. But I also knew that if I was to find any peace I had to work it through on my own. If I didn't own my thoughts for myself I would never be quite sure it was what I believed. There would always be a part of me wondering if they were

He Never Let Go

someone else's thoughts rather than my own. The problem was that I have spent so much of my life being told what to think by others at school, at nursing school and at Church that I realized it wouldn't be easy to work out what I thought for myself. But somehow I had to do it.

12

Missing God

At first I hoped that eventually I would work out what I thought about God without too much effort and that the wild variations about Him in my thoughts would cease. But it didn't appear that this would be any time soon because my thoughts were still doing a vigorous Newton's Cradle. I found it grueling. It was about this time that I realized something else, which plunged me into an even darker place than I was already in. I realized I was grieving for God. I no longer believed He was there but at the same time I missed Him so much it hurt. It was so sudden. One moment I was happy for there to be no God and the next I missed Him enormously. I was quite shocked by the unexpectedness of this new feeling. The following is a quote from my blog[13] at the time.

"Wednesday 10th November 2010 - Grieving for God

'O God, you are my God, earnestly I seek you; my soul thirsts for you, my body longs for you, in a dry and weary land where there is no water.' Psalm 63:1

I realized this afternoon that one of the feelings I have buzzing around my head is a deep

---

[13] The Patchwork Blog, http://patch-work-blog.blogspot.com

feeling of loss and grief that I don't have God anymore. I want to believe in God desperately. For most of the years I had a faith in God, he was a friend and strength through bad times. I am feeling desperately sad that deep down I no longer believe in the existence of a God. I just feel bereft. I am trying to convince myself that there is a God but deep down I just don't think I believe there is one. There is a big gaping hole where God used to be. What am I going to fill that hole with? How do I cope on my own?"

Without warning, that afternoon on November 10th 2010, I became aware of a massive void in my life: God wasn't there. I felt empty and desolate. I missed God. I yearned for Him desperately. I missed the companionship I think. That may sound an odd thing to say when talking about God but it was the sensation of always having Him there that I missed so much. He was always there in times of need. Even if He wasn't the first one I turned to He was there. I guess it had always felt like having a safety net underneath me and now that net had vanished. Well, I thought it had. I know now that He didn't leave me. It was just that I stopped being aware of Him because I didn't think He was there.

In that one moment, I realized that I wanted God back in my life. There was one mammoth obstacle though. For most of the time I didn't believe He existed. It was a very bleak, dark place in which to find myself. I was desperately yearning for someone I didn't think existed. Although I didn't know it at the time, this painful realization was the turning point in my journey through this crisis of faith. Up to that point if I am honest, a part of me was relieved to be without God. I thought I wanted to be without Him. I wanted what I thought was freedom; freedom to choose my own life. I wanted to make all my own decisions. I wanted to go where I wanted and to go there when I wanted. Until that moment having no God seemed like liberty. Suddenly, in one small second of time, I realized I missed God. Out of the blue it no longer felt like freedom that I was headed for. What I thought was total freedom to do exactly as I pleased with my life was in fact complete captivity. It felt like prison. It was a huge, dark, dank prison and I had just been sentenced to life without parole. I felt hopeless, despondent and utterly lost. I no longer felt even the slightest bit free.

At this point, I was going to the local Anglican Church on a Sunday sometimes. One Sunday the then vicar, Rev Ian Cooper, said this in a sermon,

"Once you know you are lost you are on your way to being found. If you don't know you are lost you are really lost."

This statement really spoke to me, so much so that straight away I scribbled down word for word what he had said in the back of my diary. I immediately realized this was true and it gave me a starting point. I was lost and now I knew I needed to be found. Up to this point I hadn't actually examined my beliefs during this crisis of faith. I had stopped believing in the existence of God but I hadn't looked at any theology around the issue. All I knew was that I was losing my faith and I was simply carried away with what was happening as if I was being swept out to sea on a tide that was too strong for me.

Experiencing that one moment of longing for God was enough for me to want to start trying to work out more seriously what I believed. I now had the impetus to start to look for God to see if He really existed. Although I was still experiencing the wild variations in my beliefs I thought I could now see an end in sight. One way or another I would make a definite decision about God. I just had to investigate it all from as many angles as possible. I hoped my investigation would tell me whether or not God existed.

This one moment of longing for God again also made me reconsider which church I wanted to attend. I had really appreciated the Anglican Church of the Ascension while I was there. I liked Ian, the vicar, especially his uncomplicated way of preaching, which spoke powerfully to me on more than one occasion. However, I have always liked lively, more prolonged sung worship. Worship style is very much a personal preference and no one style is either right or wrong. Some churches will put prayers and Bible readings in between each song while others will put most of the songs into one extended time of sung worship towards the beginning of the service. This latter style is more appealing to me and usually helps me become more aware of God's presence.

When I first moved to Peacehaven I had been once to a Baptist Church called Coastlands, which met in the local high school, Peacehaven Community School. I didn't continue going there after that first Sunday. I think now that subconsciously I didn't want to be in a place where I met God in sung worship. I was trying to avoid God if He was there. All the time I thought not believing in God was a kind of freedom I avoided Coastlands. I thank God for the Church of the Ascension. Their vicar was just the right person to present the truth to me once more in a non-threatening way. It was as if God had begun very gently and slowly to slip back into my consciousness without me knowing it. His church was absolutely right for me for those first few months. I started going to Coastlands when I realized I missed God because I wanted to be in a place to meet Him more powerfully if He existed. I knew from past experience that lively worship would help me.

A few days after I realized how much I was grieving for God, I found myself thinking about something I remembered Adrian Plass[14] writing. Adrian Plass is one of the most helpful Christian writers I have read. He speaks the truth with humor and a 'warts and all' honesty that I find immensely refreshing. His 'Sacred Diary' series of books are hilarious and I highly recommend them. However, I ought to give a word of warning to those of you who may be considering buying these books. The 'Sacred Diary' books are, at times, so funny that reading them on public transport will probably make you look like Jasper Carrott's 'Nutter on the Bus' (look it up on YouTube if you

---

14 Find out more about Adrian Plass and his books at http://www.adrianplass.com

have not heard this!). I found the end of 'The Theatrical Tapes of Leonard Thynn' especially side-splittingly funny and it had me crying with laughter!

Anyway, I digress (it's a bad habit). It wasn't something from one of the 'Sacred Diary' books that I had in my mind. I couldn't remember, at the time, exactly where I had read it but I remembered him writing about doubt being a regular visitor. When he comes to the door, Adrian wrote, we should allow him in but we shouldn't feed him and he'll get bored and eventually go away. I kept thinking about this over a number of days. I became aware that I had done the opposite of this. I had let doubt into my thoughts and had proceeded to feed it, water it, listen to it and chat to it for hours on end. I had stopped listening to any other voices.

I decided that if I really wanted to know what I believed about God I had to listen to all the voices in my head and not drown out some of them. It was as if until then I had been sticking my fingers in my ears and been saying loudly 'La la la, I'm not listening' every time I heard a voice that stuck up for God. Only listening to one voice is like having an orchestra with one instrument drowning out the sound of all the others. An orchestra like that wouldn't achieve its main aim of producing music for us to enjoy. An orchestra sounds infinitely better when it is conducted by someone who allows each instrument to sound at the appropriate time with the appropriate audibility and for the appropriate length of time. At this point in my journey, I decided I had to be fair to all the voices I might be hearing. I would listen to all of the instruments of the orchestra of my mind, allowing each to be more dominant in turn. As I listened I decided I would know the voice of reason when I heard it. The truth will out I thought.

I didn't know why I had been listening more to the anti-God voice than to the others. I now think it was probably anger at all the pain I wrongly perceived He had caused me by not answering my prayers for a husband and children. At the time, all I knew was that it was causing a tug of war inside me. One part of me wanted to drown out the voice of God and another part was longing and yearning for Him to be in my life again. Although I now missed God and wanted Him to exist, there was a part of me that had become totally convinced He isn't there. That part of me thought He had been never been there and that He was a myth, a lie I had believed for twenty eight years. But the part of me that was longing and yearning for Him to be in my life again hoped there was a possibility that there was a God. This part of me hoped that He would forgive me for walking away from Him and we would go back to being close once more. One small part of me wondered briefly if God were just a distant God and not interested in the world He had made but this didn't last for long. I guess that my experience prior to losing my faith counteracted the belief that God was distant.

I also flirted with the idea that there is a God but not the Christian one. This idea didn't last long either. Over the years Christianity has stood out to me from any other religion I have looked at. Forgive me if I oversimplify things but it appears to me that in all other faiths it's mostly about what we have to do to earn eternal life. God may be seen as merciful but ultimately it is how we act that gets us into heaven. In Christianity God leaves heaven in the person of Jesus and comes to earth to die in our place in order that we might be given eternal life for free. All we have to do is accept this free gift. We don't have to earn it. We then try to live a life that pleases God out of gratitude rather than to earn our place in heaven. I find that far more appealing than having to earn it all myself. In non-Christian faiths I think I would be always wondering if I were good enough, if I had done enough to get into heaven. Were the scales going to tip in my favor or not? No, if there is a God, I thought, Christianity explains who He is accurately.

So, I found myself trying to decide if there was either no God at all or if there was a God like the one I had learned about before, a God of love who wanted me to know Him as He knew me. I supposed I should be able to reason it all out if I thought about it hard enough and logically enough. I thought listening to each voice would help me to work out what each one was really saying and why it was saying it. Just wanting there to be a God who loved me wasn't enough. I didn't want to dedicate my life to a non-existent deity. If God didn't exist I'd have to grieve for Him and then just get on with my life. If He did exist I would go back to Him. So, I started on a serious search to try to work out if there is a God using reason alone.

13

Reasoning

I now felt I had a mission and it was to work out using reason alone if there is a God or not. From the time I had started losing my faith I had spent a lot of time on various websites for former Christians. They provided a place where I could be honest about my doubts and find others who had been through similar things to me. These websites now gave me a place to go to read different reasoned views about God. Many of the people on these sites seemed to use only reason and nothing else to explore the possibility of the existence of God. If their reasoning told them there couldn't be a God then they didn't believe. I decided that if reason had told these people so definitely that there was no God then I could use reason on my 'find out if there is a God' mission too. I still wanted to be true to my mission to listen to all the voices but I wanted to do it using only the filter of reason. I thought if I looked at it hard enough, I would be able to work it out logically. I could look at all the evidence and come to a sensible, reasonable conclusion about the existence of God.

So with this in mind, I read many posts and comments on various forums of these websites for former Christians. There seemed to be assorted reasons given as evidence that God does not exist. A few of them stood out to me more than some of the others did. They are as follows.

He Never Let Go

- The whole debate about whether or not the Creator of such a complex universe would need a creator Himself.
- The question of how God could allow such suffering as we see in the world
- The apparent contradiction between free will and an all-knowing God.

These things had never been an obstacle to my faith in God before but now I wondered if there was some sense in all these arguments put forward by atheists. I tried to look at these different theological arguments but I found it very hard. I can so often see all sides of an argument. When person 'A' speaks I can see the sense in what they are saying, that is until person 'B' starts saying the opposite and then I can totally understand that person as well. Maybe when it comes to peace making being able to understand all sides of an argument is a gift but it didn't help when trying to understand what I believed about God. Each voice I stopped to listen to made total sense. There wasn't a clear winner in the voices because each one sounded sensible and reasonable.

The first question in my list, 'who created God', interested me because it is a question that I had never previously considered. I always assumed God didn't need creating - He is eternal. Now I wanted to see if my long held belief on this question would be shaken if I looked at it in the light of my doubts. I had always thought that if there is a God then it stood to reason that He would be totally different to us. If He exists He can be eternal and have no beginning and no end. He doesn't need to be created. He just is. I thought it was obvious that God wouldn't be exactly like the human beings He created. We reflect Him in how we are made. We are made in His image but He is so much more than we are. Just because we can't understand how God can be eternal doesn't mean He isn't eternal. I also thought that a God I could totally understand wouldn't really be God. It would bring Him down to my level; make Him less than He is. In my mind God is someone who is greater than I am, who is wiser than I am.

I now wanted to find out if I could see this question from a different point of view, from an atheist point of view. I tried to look at it but I couldn't get past the idea that God is so 'other' than us that I can't expect to comprehend everything about Him. I still thought that if humans could completely understand God then it would mean we were equal to God. If I'm honest, I thought it was arrogant of me, a human being, to think I could understand everything about God. I realized that asking the question 'Who made God' was an unnecessary one for me. Looking at this subject made me realize that the idea of God being eternal and not having a Creator wasn't what made me stop believing in Him. I still thought that if there is a God (and at this point in my thinking it was a massive IF), then He is eternal and doesn't need a creator. My views on this hadn't changed and exploring this argument hadn't helped in my 'find out if there is a God' mission.

I thought I would look at the idea of suffering to see if that would aid me on my fact finding quest. This led on to my looking simultaneously at the question of free will as well. It was while I was looking at the issue of suffering that my ability to see something from different angles became more of a problem. Every argument I read about a loving God and suffering seemed to make sense, whichever viewpoint it was expressing.

Having said that there were some things I was sure about. I was certain that a lot of suffering is manmade and is not at all in the will of God. I was also sure that God has chosen to give us free will; He lets us make our own choices. He loves us too much to control us and make us like robots. It is our ability to choose, our having free will that makes us human. But even if God did choose to control human beings, I would have to accept He would also control me to the same degree. If that were the case He would have as much right to control my actions as He had to control people I thought were evil.

Once I started to examine the idea more I realized that I didn't have a problem with human beings being able to choose freely what they do, while at the same time believing that God is all knowing and all powerful. I think it shows that God knows us all so well that He knows what we will chose in any given situation. Maybe I am naïve in my thinking, I don't know but that is where my thoughts took me.

But these things didn't explain why nature can be so cruel with things like hurricanes, tsunamis, floods, and earthquakes. It was looking at this aspect of suffering that I found confusing. Everything I read made sense no matter what view it was expressing. I found it really hard to hear just one voice of reason. All the voices seemed reasonable to me! I tried to look at the issue and work out what I thought but I simply couldn't make a decision about it. Each article or forum post pulled me in another direction. I was back to having the Newton's Cradle in my head again. It didn't really help on my quest to discover if God existed[15].

While thinking about these things I went to a movie night at our church. The movie was called "Billy: The early years of Billy Graham" and it got me really thinking. It didn't just depict Billy Graham but also his friend Charles Templeton. Charles Templeton, like Billy Graham, was also a preacher but later became an agnostic. It was their respective reactions to the horrors of concentration camps in WWII that made me think. When seeing the unspeakable pictures of the concentration camps, Charles Templeton's reaction was to question God. 'How can a loving God allow that to happen?' seems to have been his main question. It seems to have caused too many doubts for him to cope with and eventually he stopped believing in God. But Billy Graham's response was 'But man did that not God', and it didn't seem to shake his faith much. He carried on believing in God. Both men looked at the same thing but had different reactions to it.

What makes one man doubt and one man believe when looking at the same evidence? I thought the same when reading Richard Dawkins book 'The God Delusion'

---

[15] Since returning to faith I have looked at the whole issue of suffering again and found a deeper understanding of parts of it. However, at the time I am writing about I got nowhere with my thoughts.

He Never Let Go

and then reading a book called 'The Dawkins Delusion' by Alistair McGrath. Both men seemed to point to the same evidence, for example, the nature of our universe, and find proof of their particular view from it. If men of greater learning than me, for example Billy Graham, Charles Templeton, Richard Dawkins and Alistair McGrath, couldn't agree despite all being intelligent, thinking people then what hope did I have? I could already see all sides of the argument! Every time I read a reasoned argument on one viewpoint or another I could identify with what was being said. I was beginning to doubt my ability to make a decision about God using reason alone.

The Billy Graham movie left me feeling desperately confused and not quite knowing what to do. Not only did it make me wonder if I would actually work out using reason if God existed but also it struck a deep cord in another way too. One scene of the movie that really moved me and struck a deep cord was when Charles Templeton is shown to be talking to a reporter not long before he died. At one point when referring to Jesus, he breaks down into tears and says,

"I miss him."

I have no idea how realistic that scene is; there may have been bucket loads of artistic license used in the writing of it, I don't know. But the sentiments expressed by this character in that scene reflected very closely my own feelings at the time. It left me quite drained. I was once more connecting with the part of me that badly wanted to believe in God.

I tried to succeed at my 'find out if God exists by using

reason alone' mission. I tried, I really did, but I felt as though I was going round in circles. It felt like trying to find my way through a maze. Every time I thought I had found the way and my mind had settled on there either being or not being a God I would turn the next corner to find a dead end. I then had to turn back and try another route. I simply couldn't work it out. I appeared to be failing at working it all out for myself, so I decided I needed to look at it from another angle.

I decided instead to look at Jesus because who He is depends on whether there is a God or not. If there is a God then Jesus was His son; He was God in human form. That is what I'd been taught for so many years. But if there is no God then who is Jesus? Was He simply a good man who showed us a good way to live? Jesus died when He was about thirty three years old but did He come back to life again on the third day as the Gospels describe? I found it really hard to work out who Jesus was without God. But was that my Christian background speaking? I had been a Christian for the whole of my adult life and I had only ever thought about Jesus as being the Son of the Living God, as both divine and human at the same time. It was hard to think of Him in any other way.

    I decided that the resurrection was crucial to understanding who Jesus is. I decided that if He did rise from the dead then He is God, which proved God's existence. If He didn't rise again then He wasn't God and there may not be a God. So having decided that Jesus' resurrection was key to my mission, I tried to look at that. I thought the testimony of Jesus' disciples was a useful place to start. Their behavior, as described in the New Testament, tells me that they really did believe Jesus rose from the dead. Most of the disciples were ordinary working men who were not given to fanciful invention. They were hard working people who got on with the everyday things of life. They weren't expecting the resurrection at all yet they became convinced that Jesus was alive despite having seen Him die. They believed that they had actually seen the risen Christ for themselves. They knew He was alive.

Another question that seemed important to me was this. Why would they die for something they knew to be an outright lie? If they knew Jesus hadn't really risen to life why would they lie about it? It cost most of them their lives. They were martyred for their belief that Jesus was the Son of God. It simply didn't make sense that they had made it up. They really believed Jesus had risen. But could they have been deceived about it? Perhaps Jesus wasn't really dead when he was taken down from the cross. I didn't think it likely. The apostle John was standing at the cross with Jesus' mother Mary when Jesus died. John knew that he had seen blood and water coming out of Jesus' side, which was medical proof that Jesus had really died. It meant that the blood had started to separate. It wouldn't have done this while he was still alive. Also, the Romans were very experienced executioners. I thought it unlikely they made a mistake like that. I just couldn't see down to earth fishermen like John and his friends, being easily deceived.

But if they were, who deceived them? And why?

Within weeks of the death of Jesus His disciples were causing disruption in public places, telling people that Jesus was alive and that He was the Son of God. They were healing people in Jesus' name. If the authorities had deceived the disciples all they needed to do was produce Jesus' body and this trouble would likely have stopped. They could have disproved the disciples' assertion that Jesus was alive. No, the disciples were convinced that Jesus had died and come back to life again and they weren't deceived.

Looking at the resurrection, I began to think that there might just be an end to my mission in sight. But I thought too soon. My 'I don't think there is a God' voice took over once more. This voice put up the objection that I was basing my knowledge of what both Jesus and the disciples did on the Bible accounts of the incident. If there is no God then the Bible is just another collection of writings, which may or may not be true. Indeed, at this time I thought the Bible was mostly likely to be untrue, so my above arguments on the resurrection were also likely untrue. I needed to try to work out if the Bible was true. But it seemed like an enormous task.

Then I remembered what the Alpha[16] course taught about the Bible. There was a chart in the booklet we gave out to attendees, which describes various statistics about the Bible, and other ancient writings

---

16 Alpha is a low-pressure, fun and informative course. It is a place to relax, share your thoughts and explore the meaning of life. The course is designed primarily for people who don't go to church, but are interested in the Christian faith. http://uk-england.alpha.org/

He Never Let Go

The chart gives the date that the each document was originally written and then the date that the earliest available copy today was written. The gap between these two figures is recorded in the next column along. The shorter the time between the actual writing of the document and the time of the earliest available copy we have today, the more accurate we can be sure the document is. Looking at this chart again, I could see that there is a comparatively short time lapse between the time the gospels were written and the date of the earliest available copy. It varies between 30 and 310 years depending on which part of the Gospels is being referred to. Compared with the other ancient writings shown on the chart the time lapse is nothing. The next shortest time difference was for Livy's Roman History. The earliest copy we have of that was written 900 years after it was originally written. It means that at the time the earliest available copy of the Gospels (or parts of the gospels) were written there would have been people still alive who would have experienced the Gospel events for themselves. I decided that this meant that the Gospels we have today are an accurate representation of what the writers actually wanted to say.

I confess that the thought of trying to research if this chart was accurate didn't really appeal. It seemed too huge a task. If the chart wasn't accurate then the various clergymen at Holy Trinity Brompton who developed the Alpha course over a number of years had given misleading information. I thought it unlikely that a whole team at a large, well known church would all be deliberately putting in wrong information. So, I decided that the gospels did reflect what their writers intended to say. If this was the case, then Jesus rose from the dead and He is God, so God must exist. At last, I thought I was getting somewhere.

However, it seemed to be a case of two steps forward one step backward (at least it wasn't one forward and two backward). The part of me doubting God kicked in yet again. I found myself thinking that just because the gospels reflect what the authors actually wanted to say, it doesn't mean that what they wanted to say was correct. What if the information they used to write the gospels wasn't right? Although I was leaning more towards the resurrection being true, I was not convinced enough to make a decision to return to God. There was enough doubt about the reliability of the gospel accounts in my mind to prevent the resurrection being the definitive proof I was looking for. I'd come to another dead end in the maze of my thoughts, although perhaps with this dead end I was nearer to the centre of the maze than I had been previously. But it still felt as if the more I looked at things, the less able I felt to make a decision.

As I've said before I found that as I looked at various pieces of evidence I could see both sides of the argument. I couldn't decide what the truth was. My mind spun. My mission to discover the truth of God's existence using reason alone wasn't working the way I thought it would. I was constantly hitting dead ends. I was rushing head long into brick walls. Where was I going wrong? Other ex-Christians seemed to be so sure, using reason alone, that

He Never Let Go

there was not a God. Why did it all seem so complicated to me? I thought once I started looking at things in a reasonable, logical way it would become clear but if anything it was the opposite. I desperately wanted to know the truth. I needed to know if believing in the existence of God meant I believed in a lie. If God really was there I wanted to know. I wanted to know the truth and I wanted to be able to reason my way to that truth but I simply couldn't do it. The more I tried the more I ended up banging my poor sore head against the brick wall of reason.

14

A wider search

It was about this time that I remembered essays we wrote while I was in training with Church Army. One type of essay was called a Practical Theology Report (PTR for the inevitable shorthand). We wrote these essays while we were on our practical placements. Practical placements were when we spent between four and six weeks working in a church or Christian outreach setting, gaining practical experience in evangelistic ministry. A PTR was a written exploration from a theological perspective of a situation we had come across or something that had happened to us while we were on our placement. In other words, we needed to try to work out what God would have thought about such a situation. We were required to look at this event using Scripture, reason, experience, and tradition to help us. We used Scripture to find out what the Bible told us. We then applied logic and reason to the situation and looked at it through the lens of our own experience to see if that expanded our knowledge and understanding of the situation. Finally, we used tradition to find out what other Christians down the ages have thought.

I wrote one PTR about how I felt after seeing two very different ways of approaching the public reading of Scripture in two churches I attended one Sunday. In the morning I was at an Anglo-Catholic church that used a lot of ritual in how the reading from one of the gospels was performed. At the other church it was very informal indeed. The contrast interested me greatly and in my essay I wrote about Jesus' attitude to the Bible and how we can emulate it. Investigating this incident from the different approaches of Scripture, reason, tradition, and experience helped me to come to a place of more appreciation of the Bible. It helped me to have a less narrow view of the initial incident than I would have had without the study of it from different viewpoints. Had I not had to write this essay I would have probably been more judgmental about those who use more ritual. Looking at it in an open way helped me to see the deep reverence they have towards the Word of God and so I adjusted my own attitude accordingly.

I now wondered if I could use this same process in looking at the existence of God. I was beginning to realize that in using only reason I was limiting the source of information. I knew I wanted to look at things from all perspectives, not missing out any voice that might help me on my mission. I had been using only reason, albeit reason from different angles, so I decided to try to use Scripture, experience and tradition in addition to reason. I wasn't confident that it would help but I went ahead and starting looking at things from these angles as well.

I decided to start this part of my search in Scripture but I couldn't find much in it about not believing in the existence of God. In fact, the whole Bible assumes the existence of God. It starts with the words,

"In the beginning God . . ." (Genesis 1:1).

Right from the beginning of the Bible God is mentioned and His existence is not questioned. All I could see about not believing in the existence of God was in Psalm 14:1 (and Psalm 53:1). It says,

"The fool says in his heart, 'There is no God.'".

There was much more about disobeying God or doubting some aspect of God's character but not believing that He was there at all didn't seem to be covered further than that one verse. Psalm 14 goes on to say,

"They are corrupt, their deeds are vile; there is no one who does good."

The fool talked about in verse one seemed to be someone who deliberately sins and wants to do evil. It didn't seem to be talking about someone with a genuine concern about God's existence, and who would love there to be a God to follow, which is where I placed myself.

There are passages of Scripture in which God is proving He is ultimately the One with all the power and knowledge. In Job chapters 38 to 42 God is speaking to Job and convincing him by looking at different aspects of creation that He knows what He is doing. However, Job's problem was not one of disbelief in the existence of God. In fact in the midst of all his suffering Job still says,

"I know that my Redeemer lives." (Job 19:25)

Job continued to believe in God despite all that went wrong in his life. No, I wouldn't get my answers from Job.

So far my looking at Scripture had simply shown me that the Bible believes God exists, which I had worked out all by myself anyway. Obviously the Bible states that there is a God because it describes itself as God's Word. The whole Bible is about God. That is why it was written, to tell us about God. Paul in 2 Timothy 3:16 says,

"All Scripture is God-breathed."

Well, it would describe itself as God-breathed wouldn't it? That didn't really help me in my quest for the truth. I didn't learn any more than I had beforehand, i.e. if there is a God then Scripture is God's Word but if there is no God then it is not God's Word.

As far as tradition went, I wanted to see if others had stopped believing in the existence of God and had come back to faith again. I had read of many ex-Christians but not really of any who had come back to faith again. I wanted to be able to read of people who had had a similar crisis of faith to me. I wanted to read about people who had come back to faith as well as those who hadn't. I wanted to be able to read about both sides of the argument. The absence of this kind of testimony made me wonder if it meant that God didn't exist. If everyone who had a crisis about the existence of God ended up ceasing to believe in Him, did that mean He wasn't there to be found? I knew that some people went through experiences when God no longer appeared to be there. Was that the same ceasing to believe in the existence of God? Was feeling the absence of God the same as what I was experiencing?

I had all these questions and no answers to them. Did it mean I was stupid and simply not intelligent enough to work it all out? If I were cleverer, I thought briefly, I would be able to reason to myself more adequately that there is no God. I dismissed that idea quite quickly. I concluded that if the reasoning of an intelligent person always led them to working out the 'truth' that there is no God then no intelligent, reasoning, person would continue to believe in God. However, not all intelligent people are atheists. Some very intelligent and reasoning people believe in the existence of God, e.g. C. S. Lewis, John Stott, and Francis Morris (who used to head up the Human Genome Project). These intelligent reasoning Christians were a stumbling block to my throwing myself wholeheartedly into atheism (something for which I now really do praise God). They sowed the seed of doubt in my unbelief about God. I began to wonder if there was something else happening deep in my subconscious mind. Were there other reasons for my not believing in God? I began to wonder if a part of me wanted there to be no God, while another part of me wanted desperately for there to be one. Maybe it was my changing desires about the existence of God that caused my thoughts to fluctuate so much.

Scripture hadn't proved beneficial in helping me decide about God's existence and tradition was only marginally more helpful than that, so I turned to look at my experience of God. The first experience that came to my mind was one I'd had back in the late 1990's. I was in a meeting at the church I attended at that time, which was being led by a visiting preacher from USA. After a time of teaching (for the life of me I can't remember what this man preached about) there came a time of prayer. I stood in line to receive prayer and a man from my congregation came to pray for me. At this time, a lot of us at the Church had been so overcome with the power of God at various meetings that we had fallen over. Although some people at that church frequently 'fell over in the Spirit'[17] when prayed for it's not something that has happened to me very often, now or then. In fact, I usually fought it and stood rooted to the spot determined that I would stay upright. I wanted to make sure that if I went down it was because God had caused it not because I had allowed myself to fall to look like God had touched me. Besides, it has always struck me as an external experience and I was more concerned with the long-term effects on me of any prayer I received. I wasn't looking for a short-term experience.

When the man from my church prayed for me that evening he didn't even touch me. In other words, unlike some people, he didn't put his hand on my head or on my shoulders. He simply prayed a short prayer that God would come to me. He prayed and I fell over. Perhaps the phrase I crumpled in a heap on the floor would be a better description. The power of God was so strong that I didn't have the chance to resist falling over as I usually did. As I lay there, I started to whimper. I was thinking in my head 'don't leave me' over and over again. Witnesses later confirmed that the only sounds I made out loud were the whimpering and no words. According to our Church leader's wife, the visiting speaker apparently heard my whimper and immediately left the person with whom he was praying. He marched straight over to me and ordered

---

[17] I am implying no particular theology about this experience by this choice of phrase for it

a 'spirit of abandonment' to leave me. Instantly I found myself screaming. It was something I had absolutely no control over. It was as if the scream was coming from the depths of my being. The scream was so intense, and so loud, that I had pinpricks of blood around my eyes afterwards. The speaker then left me with church members praying for me while he returned to the person with whom he had originally been praying. Once he had finished ministering to this person he came back to me and talked to me for a while reassuring me of God's love for me.

This experience now came back to me constantly. I had so many questions about it. Was what happened from God? Did God release me from something that day? If it was God then obviously He exists. If it wasn't God, then what was it? I know I wasn't talking aloud when I kept saying to myself 'please don't leave me'. Outwardly, I was whimpering. Eyewitnesses confirm that it was my whimper that got the speaker's attention. They tell me that his reaction was immediate. As soon as he heard the sound I was making he left the person with whom he was praying and came over to me. I am not someone who regularly falls to the floor and starts screaming when I am prayed for. It was completely out of character. I am the kind of person who is suspicious of that behavior. Was it just a coincidence that the speaker talked about a 'spirit of abandonment' in his prayer while I lay there repeating over and over in my head 'please don't leave me'?

After that strange experience, I felt much more confident in God's ongoing love for me. I was no longer afraid of Him walking away from me. It had the long term effect I wanted. It wasn't just a short term experience. Things like this experience made me think there must be a God. Mind you, a part of me still thought that maybe there was a rational explanation for this incident. It was just that I couldn't think of one. Finding a reasonable explanation for this experience that didn't involve God had me completely stumped. I suspected that atheists would probably have some kind of psychological explanation for it that I hadn't been able to work out.

Looking at my previous experience of God proved more helpful than Scripture and tradition had been. It seemed to be making the possibility of there being a God more real again. There had been a gradual shift in my thinking while I had been looking at God's existence through the lens of my old Practical Theology Reports.

Christmas 2010 was the first Christmas for ages that I didn't have to work at all. I haven't had many Christmases where I haven't worked because most of my life I have been nursing or working with the Church and both careers involve working on Christmas Day. Christmas 2010 was amazing. It was a four-day weekend. Christmas Day and Boxing Day were on a Saturday and Sunday, so we got the Monday and Tuesday off as well. It turned out to be the first Christmas for ages that I had felt able to think about the real meaning behind the celebrations.

I spent it with Elsa (my prayer partner mentioned in chapter eight) and her family. I was able to be there from Christmas Eve rather than having to rush over at lunchtime on Christmas day itself. This meant I could be there for the excitement of small children hanging up stockings for Santa Claus on the banister. It is always lovely to spend Christmas with children! There were stockings for Mummy, Daddy, and Tita[18] Lynda as well as for the children and I received a lovely gift of a necklace from Santa that year. The best gift that year though was time to think through the real meaning of Christmas. I had space to think about God.

Having 'flu after Christmas meant I had plenty of time to think things through. It was during this time I came to a major crossroads in my thoughts about God. I realized my decision to use Scripture, experience, and tradition, as well as reason in my search for the truth had confirmed something to me. I realized I could neither prove God nor disprove God using just reason while remaining open to the possibility that He is there. I never dreamed while sitting doing these Practical Theology Reports in college that they would turn out to be so valuable to me. I didn't necessarily enjoy doing them at the time. I didn't find them easy to do and I was under pressure to get them done within a certain time frame. Back then, I couldn't imagine a time when they would be seriously useful. But they were not only useful but turned out to be vital in my eventual return to God. Looking at the whole issue of whether there is a God or not from all these perspectives led me to realize something very significant. I realized the vital importance of faith when it comes to thinking about God.

---

18 Tita is Tagalog (Filipino) for Aunty and is what Elsa's children call me because being Filipino by birth it is her first language.

15

Rediscovering faith

By now I had realized that when I disregarded all but reason in trying to work out if God is there, I was in effect already deciding that He is not there. It was almost as if I had to work out what I believed about God's existence in advance in order to know whether or not to use certain ways of interpreting the evidence. Someone might say that looking at my experience was assuming an existence of God and should be avoided if I wanted to make a reasoned decision. But excluding experience assumes the non-existence of God. I decided I wasn't going to exclude a way of looking at evidence simply because it assumed an existence of God. If God is real then Scripture, spiritual experience and Christian tradition become valid ways of finding out more about Him. If I had shut the door on those things I would have already decided that God is not real and that struck me as being very biased to one view. I wanted to be truly open one way or the other about there being a God. I wanted to consider things from all angles. I wanted to put aside my conflicting desires and just seek the truth in as open a way as I could.

I can understand why some people want to use just reason to seek God. At a human level it was natural for me to assume I could find out if there is a God or not using just reason. Looking at all points of view logically should show one way or another if there is a God or not. But for me it didn't. I couldn't work out which reasoned argument was correct. I wanted to follow the truth but I couldn't work out what that truth was by just reasoning it out in my mind.

I realized something else too. In using only reason I was assuming that God is like human beings. I was assuming that everything about Him is to be understood in the same way as I understand another person. But God is not like us. He is other than us. He is God. If there is a God then His being eternal for example would be natural. If I say that God cannot be eternal because that is impossible then I am applying human characteristics to Him. If there is a God then He is different to us. We reflect Him in some ways but He is so much more than we are. I realized that the folk I came across on the websites for former Christians often applied human characteristics to God and didn't allow for Him being different to us. In some ways I think it is arrogant for us to assume it is possible for a human being to understand all there is know about God. It takes God's divinity away from Him.

By this stage I hadn't made the leap to believing there is a God. I had just decided that if there is a God then it stood to reason I had to use all manner of ways of seeking Him. I decided that if He is there He is creator and I am creation. Therefore, He is greater than I am; He isn't exactly the same as me. If He were there, as far as I was able, I would allow Him to be God and not try to squeeze Him into a human mould. I wanted to be open to the truth as it really is, not the truth as I would like it to be.

He Never Let Go

My wanting to look at things in this open way made me realize something else. I was coming round to the fact that if there is a God, then faith must be involved in how we approach Him, and how we decide He is there. If there is a God, then I have to use faith in every aspect of my relationship with Him. God is not human and He can't be accessed in normal human ways. I can't pick up the phone and dial His number, or pop over for a cup of tea and a chat. Yes, we are made in His image, but that means we reflect Him in all aspects of who we are. It doesn't mean we are exactly the same as Him. If there is a God, then He is beyond our human understanding because He is Spirit and not human. If we want to know what this God is like we can look to Jesus, who is God in human form. But God is more than the incarnation of Himself that is Jesus. He is the Holy Trinity, God in three persons. The Father and the Holy Spirit do not have human form. It is because of this 'otherness' of God that the Bible is full of instructions about having faith. We need it to take on board that God is there and that He cares for us.

I also reflected that there is very little in life we can be one hundred percent sure of by reason alone. We often have to use faith in choosing what to do. To a certain extent, I use faith every day. When I get in my car, I have faith that other drivers will stop when there is a red light. Sometimes they don't, but mostly they do. The fact that some drivers don't stop at a red light doesn't mean I stop trusting the lights as a way to drive on our roads. It means I follow the traffic laws myself and keep a close look out for what is going on around me. Even in our law courts in

Britain, a jury is expected to find someone guilty 'beyond all reasonable doubt'. There is an element of accepting that the jury can't always be 100% certain of what happened in any situation. We use reason but accept that there is a limit to our reason.

By now I was beginning to accept the idea that there is a limit to my reason when dealing with God. My reason told me some things but there were other things that I couldn't work out with reason alone. When I arrived at this point the burden became considerably lighter. It was as if I had been struggling up a large, steep hill until that point and now I had got to the peak. It was another turning point. Now it was downhill all the way!

I realized a mixture of faith and reason is acceptable. I recalled what happened when St Thomas first heard Jesus had risen from the dead. This event is recorded by the apostle John in John 20:24-29.

"Now Thomas (also known as Didymus), one of the Twelve, was not with the disciples when Jesus came. So the other disciples told him, 'We have seen the Lord!' But he said to them, 'Unless I see the nail marks in his hands and put my finger where the nails were, and put my hand into his side, I will not believe.' A week later his disciples were in the house again and Thomas was with them. Though the doors were locked, Jesus came and stood among them and said, 'Peace be with you!' Then he said to Thomas, 'Put your finger here; see my hands. Reach out your hand and put it into my side. Stop doubting and believe'. Thomas said to him, 'My Lord and my God!' Then Jesus told him, 'Because you have seen me, you have

believed; blessed are those who have not seen and yet have believed.'"

    I saw something in this story now that I hadn't seen before. Jesus met Thomas where he was. The second time Jesus appeared to the disciples, he told Thomas to put his hand in his side, to stop doubting and to believe. Like Thomas I had been refusing to believe. I had doubted. I knew now that if God existed, if Jesus was indeed divine, that he wouldn't reprimand me. He would meet me where I was. I could almost see him as he simply held out his hands and showed me his side just as he had for Thomas. Jesus allowed Thomas to use reason to get to a point of faith. I knew now that I didn't have to work it all out with reason. Faith was a legitimate follow on from reason. Now I hoped I could do the same as Thomas had. Once I got to this point in my thoughts the next step towards the return of my faith came quickly.

In fact, it was within days at the beginning of January 2011. I was sitting at my computer re-reading my blog posts from a blog[19] I had started back in November. I was reminding myself of all I had learned over the preceding few months when it suddenly hit me. Faith is something I needed to choose to do. I didn't need to wait to feel the faith. If I did that it would be a very long wait. I could make up my mind, as an act of my will, to have faith there is a God. When I chose to take that step of faith into the unknown I had no certainty God was there.

---

19 The Patchwork Blog, http://patch-work-blog.blogspot.com

It was like the scene from the movie 'Indiana Jones and the Last Crusade' when Indy steps off a cliff into a great chasm in the rock. He is following instructions in a special notebook. It tells him to step off the canyon into what appears to be thin air. After a few moments of mental preparation, he makes a choice and steps off the edge of the canyon. And he doesn't fall. He looks down at his feet. At this point in the movie the camera pans out and we see the scene from a different viewpoint. We see that there is a bridge made of rock across the canyon. By following the directions in the book, Indy has stepped onto a bridge that was invisible from where he was standing.

I felt like that sitting at my computer that day. I was stood in front of an invisible bridge across the canyon of doubt. My heart was beating a little faster and there was a strange feeling in the pit of my stomach. 'Am I doing the right thing?' I thought as I sat there. I knew I wanted to make the decision but it would take courage. Before I could change my mind again, I made a decision, took a step of faith, and prayed out loud.

"God I am choosing to believe that you are real and that you are here. I choose once more to believe that you exist."

I decided as an act of my will that there is a God and I was going to have faith in Him. It was a conscious act of my will and my mind. At the time I said those words to myself and to God I wasn't feeling faith at all. In fact I felt nothing but uncertainty and doubt.

However, after I made the decision as an act of my will, I felt a huge sense of peace. The peace of God flooded once more into my empty heart. It was such a relief. I can't begin to tell you! I was then reminded of what happened when the Israelites crossed the River Jordan into the Promised Land. The river didn't part for them to cross until after the priests at the front of the line stepped into the water. They had to step into the river before the miracle occurred. We read in Joshua 3:15-16.

"Yet as soon as the priests who carried the ark reached the Jordan and their feet touched the water's edge, the water from upstream stopped flowing. It piled up in a heap a great distance away."

The river Jordan of doubt in my mind had just parted and I could now cross over into faith once more. A massive sense of relief surged through me as I realized God was there. He had not left me. He was still there and encouraging my every step forward.

16

An old, new christian

At first, once my faith returned I thought everything would jump straight back to what it was beforehand. How wrong can you be? I'd made a leap of faith into the unknown and found God once more but I soon realized that my faith was different. In fact it was a very weird sensation. I had all the head knowledge and experience of someone who had been a Christian for twenty seven years and who had ten years of training and ministry with Church Army but my heart and my spirit were like those of a new Christian. I was an old, new Christian. I felt disjointed somehow as if parts of me were foreign and not really me.

Initially I slipped into 'teacher mode' with myself and tried to lecture myself back to what I once was. I thought that now I knew God existed again everything else about my faith would be the same as it had been prior to my crisis but that wasn't the case. I re-read familiar passages in the Bible, expecting something to click back immediately into traditional evangelical mode but it didn't. Every so often that inner, and sometimes judgmental, teacher voice of mine would tell me off for not being what I previously was. I'd tell myself I had to get back to believing everything I used to believe immediately if not sooner.

He Never Let Go

It took a few weeks but I gradually realized that this was unhelpful. It made me want to run away from God again. Gradually, I learned to recognize and ignore this destructive voice. It was scary to think that I lived with this inner voice nearly all the time before I lost my faith. No wonder I lost my faith when I came up against a pain I couldn't handle. There was no grace or mercy in the way I spoke to myself. I am now sure that this inner voice wasn't God. God is love and His voice of correction is spoken without condemnation. My inner voice was so often one of judgment and condemnation.

I can remember going to a Bible study group again for the first time. I was very nervous about it. I didn't know how I would react. To make matters worse I got lost on the way there. I think my nerves affected my sense of direction! So when I arrived I was quite emotional. It felt familiar in a way, to be sat with a group of friendly welcoming Christians reading the Bible. But in another way I felt like an alien.

One part of me wanted to pretend I didn't know anything. My faith felt so new I didn't want to be put in a place of being someone with the knowledge of the Bible. I didn't want to be the one with the answers. I wanted to be free to have big questions about God. I'd had enough of having to say out loud one thing about God while believing another inside while I was still ministering at Christ Church Turnham Green in Chiswick.

But also that judgmental voice was still there whispering in my ear. It was telling me to just pull myself together and get on with being a mature Christian. It was such an unhelpful voice. Being judgmental is never helpful.

It doesn't draw people towards knowing God. It normally pushes them away from God. If you read the Gospels, you will see that Jesus was not judgmental with people. He was loving. He challenged people, yes, but with compassion and always knowing how to challenge without judging. I needed to learn to be like that with myself.

In the end, I told myself that the leap into believing in God's existence again was just the first step on my way back to God. I had to keep taking little steps after that: no taking great big giant strides. It was an important step in my return to God. I came to understand that I mustn't rush things and decided to take it very slowly. I wanted to take each new step as it appeared, rather than going looking for it before I was ready. I wanted to sit for a while with each new thought. I wanted to take in what had happened and what I was feeling about it all. This was where my blog[20] came in handy. It was very helpful in enabling me to work out what I was thinking and feeling.

---

[20] The Patchwork Blog, http://patch-work-blog.blogspot.com

17

Doubt: friend or foe

Jude 22 *"be merciful to those who doubt"*

Once I started to take things slowly like this it didn't take me long to realize that I had some questions buzzing around my head. They were questions that I hadn't really asked myself before. The foremost question I had was about doubt. My faith had started to change and my inner judgmental voice had started to soften. My faith now was changing into something more real than it had been previously. One of the main transformations was my response to the presence of doubt in my life. Before this crisis I clung to my faith with as a way of proving to myself that it was true. I didn't want to ask questions about it. I felt threatened by them. I thought 'Of course I believe. I believe wholeheartedly', and that was without question most of the time.

But now I began to see that my faith in its new form is quite distinct to what it once was. My faith now feels like faith whereas before my crisis it was more like blind acceptance. I hadn't looked at the negatives, the questions, and the doubts about what I believed. To a certain extent I was just living the way I have been told to live by someone else, and believing most of what they told me. Now I was working it all out for myself. It was about this time that I was struck powerfully by something my friend Dr. Richard Goode said on his blog[21],

"I was once told 'my boy, always preach your convictions not your questions'. But I had seen what convictions can do to a spirit and I lived by one truth alone; 'treasure the questions'. Even in those days I was learning that certainty was the armor put on by those who had yet to gain the courage to live by faith."

I could see now what Richard was saying. Somehow the presence of questions and doubt has made my faith more faith-like. By that I mean I am now letting the questions sit comfortably side by side with faith that God is who He says He is in the Bible. As the Adrian Plass quote I mentioned in chapter twelve suggests, I allow doubt (and his friend questions) to come in and sit in a corner when they come knocking at the door. I acknowledge they are there but I still have faith. I still believe. I am learning to live with them. Sometimes they get up and leave for a while but then they return. And so it goes on. That for me is faith. If I had answers to all my questions, I wouldn't need faith. There will come a time when we go to heaven that we will have our questions answered. We will meet God face to face and faith will become complete knowledge. Until that time I have faith despite the questions and doubt. In St Paul's second letter to the Corinthians (2 Corinthians 4:7-9) he says,

"We are hard pressed on every side, but not crushed;

---

[21] From The Churchless Sexton's blog post, 'The last time I stood in a pulpit' http://www.myspace.com/richardgoode/blog. Used with kind permission.

perplexed, but not in despair; persecuted, but not abandoned; struck down, but not destroyed."

The word perplex seems to imply that Paul also had times of being unsure or uncertain, times when he had doubts and questions about life, God, or faith but he still chose to believe. Since coming out of my crisis of faith it has hit me more clearly every day that the opposite of faith is not doubt. The opposite of faith is certainty. Richard's words about questions, certainty, and faith had struck home powerfully. Certainty is misunderstanding the real nature of faith.

My faith, before I experienced this absence of belief in God, was certainty with no room for questions. I was scared of the questions. Certainty was like a veil I hid behind to protect myself from having to step out in faith. When I hit a major problem in my life, my faith hadn't been stretched enough to deal with it. It crumpled under the strain.

My return to believing in God's existence came when I allowed myself to stop looking for absolute proof and simply accepted as an act of my will that God existed. It is this willingness to allow doubt, uncertainty, and unanswered questions to live side by side with faith that enabled me to return to Jesus. Not only did it allow me to return to faith but it also made my faith far deeper and stronger. Maybe going through a time of great testing of our faith is necessary for it to develop into something better. Others on the websites for former Christians seem to get stuck on this point. They need absolute proof and in the absence of this they didn't believe.

Lynda Alsford

In February 2011, I heard a lovely, wise Roman Catholic Priest talk about how the light can be more appreciated when you know the darkness. I think I am beginning to realize that for myself. I have now experienced the darkness of believing there is no God. I know what it is to have only a deep, dark, empty, void where my faith used to be. I know what it is to have no anchor for my life. Having this experience means that the faith I now have seems even more precious to me. The light of faith is so much brighter than it was before. It's only a small beginning but I am beginning to see the value of questions and doubt. I know I will go on learning more. My faith will go on being stretched.

18

Church: support or idol

Another question I had was about the role of the church in my life. I never completely stopped going to Church during my crisis of faith. Until I had made a total commitment to atheism (which thankfully I never did) I wanted to keep some level of input about faith. It was important to me not to disregard any one viewpoint. Had I stopped going to church completely I would not have had the input about faith from a Christian perspective. However, I was no longer committed to a particular church once I moved away from London and from church ministry. I started off going to the Anglican Church, The Church of the Ascension. After a few months I moved to Coastlands Church, a Baptist church that meets in the local High School. I had a warm welcome and met some lovely people in both churches. I went along to most of the Sunday services but I didn't commit myself to anything more than that.

In the weeks after I returned to faith, I realized that I wanted more Christian input than just attending the Sunday service. I decided to join a midweek Bible study group again. I found I was missing sharing things with other Christians and wanted to build closer relationships with some of the people at my new church. Since being in Peacehaven I had made a lot of non-Christian friends and I loved it. However, there are times when I want to share things with other people who have a faith. I chose a home group that had other single women in it as well as a married couple.

The thought of joining a home group made me feel unexpectedly nervous and vulnerable. I was somewhat surprised by it because I am very used to being in a small group setting. I enjoy being with people and I'm used to sharing what I think with others. As I tried to work out the reason for my apprehension I began to realize that opening up to someone in my role as an evangelist had given me something to hide behind. I always had my 'member of staff' hat on and I was always conscious that people were looking to me as an example. This time I was just me being me. I had no role to hide behind. I've found over the years that making myself vulnerable as a minister of religion, by being open about some of my spiritual battles, helped others on a similar journey. But there was always a limit to how vulnerable I would make myself. For example, I hadn't felt able to get up and say from the pulpit, 'I think I am losing my faith, I don't think there is a God anymore'. There was always the worry that if I did that I would lose my job, and therefore my home too. I was being vulnerable within certain parameters. There was a safety to it. I knew from experience that it helped people, so it made me popular which is, I guess, what I was craving to a certain extent.

Now it was just me, myself, and I. I had no role as a lay minister to hide behind. My faith was still wobbly, like a toddler who has only just learned to walk. I was no longer coming from a place of unshakeable faith in what the Bible said. I was still recovering from the fact that I had been through a really dark valley of doubt and had almost become an atheist. It was a scary place and opening up from this position felt very different to opening up as I had done before. Going to Bible studies as a minister meant I could hide behind my knowledge and I didn't have to think about things on a personal level. I just spoke on auto pilot a lot of the time. Now I wanted to really grapple and be honest about things. Not that I had been consciously dishonest beforehand, not until I lost my faith anyway.

When it came to going to the new home group I found it challenging. Fortunately, the members of the group were really welcoming and I enjoyed their company a great deal. However, it was harder than I expected to leave behind all the knowledge I had acquired as an evangelist. I was aware that previously so much of my faith had been from my head and I knew I now needed to learn at a heart level. What I didn't need was to gain more head knowledge. I needed to be honest about what I thought deep down and not just give the answer I thought I ought to. But old habits die hard! Once I was in the group, I felt almost as though I didn't know how to act. Part of me wanted to speak from my head knowledge as I always had done and part of me wanted to let out what was in my heart.

It wasn't long before I found myself leading our Bible study group one Tuesday evening. It scared me how quickly I fell back into asking questions of people, trying to get them to engage with what we were reading. At the time I acted spontaneously to the situation and it felt OK doing it. I was back on auto-pilot. I reacted almost subconsciously. Later that evening when I got home, I felt very vulnerable and scared in a strange way. I couldn't put my finger on what was wrong at the time. I just knew that I didn't want to get back to where I was before. I didn't want to slip back into answering everything out of head knowledge and not engaging my heart. I wanted this time to be a real heart response to God, to discover Him without being told what to think or believe. I didn't have someone actually telling me out loud what I should believe. It was just that being in the role of leading a study again made me automatically hear inside my head all the words of my training and my knowledge.

It was almost like being on a roller coaster. I got on without realizing what I was doing and then I was scared that I wouldn't be able to get back off. I found myself without warning on a roller coaster ride of emotions about being so involved in a small church group.

The people at Coastlands church are lovely and I enjoy their company. The leaders at that time, Clive and Debby are lovely and I really appreciated their ministry. There are some truly special people there but when I started attending it, the overall effect was much the same as many churches I have been a part of before. It was still Church, a good Church, an understanding Church but still Church. I seemed to have a battle going on inside me. A part of me wanted to get back into being committed to a church and helping as much as I could as I had done before at other churches. But another part of me hated the thought of it. That part of me felt as if I was being dragged back into a swamp of church commitments again. I hadn't long left a job where Church commitments took over my life and I lost sight of God. I wasn't ready to jump back into the same thing again.

I didn't want to be back in the situation where I was trying to make my faith fit what others say. I wanted to work out a relationship with God on my own. I felt it was vital that my faith was strongly based in God alone with support from others, rather than being a faith in the church with God helping, which is what I now think had been the case prior to my crisis. I knew I wanted God to remain the main focus of my life not church.

These thoughts led me to look at this question in a different way. Have I made Church an idol? Sometimes when writing my blog people would kindly leave comments about it for me. One such comment came someone responding to my blog post about how I had felt uncomfortable and very vulnerable leading the Bible study group. She asked the question,
"I am wondering why you are doing what clearly makes you feel uncomfortable."

The inquirer put into words a question that was sitting on the edges of my sub-conscious. Why indeed was I feeling the pull to be very involved in a church again? When I left Christ Church I knew I needed plenty of time away from Church commitments to work things out between God and myself. Now I had found myself jumping back into the deep end again and I wanted to work out why.

Once I started to think about this question I realized I was getting Church and God mixed up somehow. It was as though I had been worshiping Church not God. I thought that being a Christian meant I had to get very involved in my local Church and I had no choice about it. It was as if God was the church and the church was God. God supported me in my worship and dedication to the local Church rather than it being the other way round as it should. I decided I needed to rethink my role as a Christian in the local church – on a temporary basis at least. It's almost as if being a 'good' member of the church and being approved of by them was more important than spending time with God and building up my relationship with Him again. I felt I couldn't separate God from the local Church.

I had made this leap of faith, and I had chosen to believe in God again. However, for some reason I was trying to go back to what it was like before, despite having worked out how negative an effect that had on my personal walk with Jesus. I had started to believe in God again but then my focus had moved away from God and onto Church. I knew I needed to start as I meant to go on and worship God first, not Church. I was reminded of the Westminster Confession, which says,

"Man's chief end is to glorify God, and to enjoy him forever."

I knew I needed to concentrate on enjoying God. I also knew that if I didn't make God my first priority, I would end up burnt out as I had been before. I knew I needed to learn to get a balance between loving God and building my relationship with Him, and my need to be involved in the local Church. I was scared by how fast it was veering back to being tipped in favor of Church again and I knew I had to pull back. I had made a step of faith by choosing to believe once more in God and He must come first. It is God who gives me eternal life not the Church. It's Jesus who died for me not the Church. Church and fellow Christians should be a support to my faith in God (and all this means for reaching out to others). They shouldn't be the focus of my faith.

I want to clarify I didn't want to stop going to Church. I wanted to have a group of fellow Christians I could worship with because I feel closer to God when I am worshipping Him with others who also love Him. I wanted a small group of Christians to whom I am accountable i.e. my home group. My home group host calls our group 'the family group'. I love that idea of being part of a family with them, especially as I live alone. These things build me up in God. What I want to avoid is these things taking over completely and God getting pushed out of the picture.

I don't think I realized before how much my faith was tied up in what I did at Church. Even as I write this I realize even more how much my being accepted by the local Church was confused in my mind with being accepted by God. Church had become my God. Being involved with the Church and caring what the Church thought of me was my idol. Now I want God to be my God not Church. I am learning to spend time with God for His sake, not for how Church will view me. It has been an exciting, if somewhat bumpy journey!

19

Why me?

Normally when I ask the question 'Why me?' it is out of self-pity. It is from an 'O woe is me' sort of an attitude. This time it was different. The question wasn't arising from an attitude of self-pity. It was from a feeling of profound gratitude. I was trying to work out why I had returned to faith, having been to a point of virtual atheism, while so many others who stop believing in God don't return to faith.

I know God wants everyone who goes through a time of doubting and disbelief to come back to Him but not everyone chooses to do so. Experiencing the futility of trying to reason God into existence led me firmly to taking a step of faith once more into the arms of God. Some see it is impossible to prove God with reason alone and as a result believe wholeheartedly that it means there is no God. I realize I may be oversimplifying their arguments and I apologize if I am but I think they believe that if there is a God then reason alone should be able to prove His existence. When it doesn't they see no option but to deduce that there is no God.

I saw the futility of using reason to prove God and came eventually to the conclusion that this fact doesn't mean there is no God. This discovery freed me to make a leap of faith, no longer restrained by having to 'prove' God.

He Never Let Go

It meant I was free to take that leap of faith without definitive scientific proof that God exists. Being unable to prove God with reason alone meant I was now free to consider other evidence of God's existence as well. In addition to reason, I could now use scripture, my experience, the experience of others, and the tradition of faith communities down the ages in my search for God. This meant God was once more within my reach. I found the discovery of the futility of reason infinitely liberating, while others find it leads them to believe just as wholeheartedly that there is no God. The ex-Christians that I met on the internet were totally committed to their view that if it doesn't stand up to reason then it isn't true. They liken my leap of faith to a belief in magic, saying I wanted there to be a God so I invented one. They simply couldn't understand my return to faith.

I realize now that when I used reason before my crisis of faith it was to justify a pre-existing belief. I would have said then I was proving God's existence and that's why I followed Him. I now see that I wasn't proving God but justifying my own pre-existing beliefs. I wonder how often others are doing the same thing whether they are atheists, agnostics, Christians, or people of other faiths. We each justify our pre-existing beliefs using reason. It was only when I was trying to be truly open to all possibilities that reason becoming a stumbling block.

My big question remains 'Why me? Why did I return to faith?' Is it that I wanted to believe in Him, given that I had missed Him and grieved for Him so much? My missing God did play a big part in how things turned out for me but missing God doesn't always cause people to turn back to Him. I have read testimonies on the internet of former Christians who miss God, who grieve for Him still but seem unable to make that leap of faith. They have not come to the same conclusion as I have and it puzzles me.

I think part of the reason for my return to faith is choices I made along the way. Choices that included things like continuing to go to church sometimes, using my old PTR essays to shape my thinking, aiming to be as open to all possibilities as I could and a desire to really seek the truth about God's existence. I kept the possibility of God existing firmly alive in my mind. I didn't close the door totally. I didn't assume automatically that I was right in saying there was no God. I knew I believed there was no God but I wanted to make sure I was right before I finally closed that door. I didn't listen to the first thought about God not existing and believe it wholeheartedly. I examined it first before making such a major decision. I am so thankful that I didn't shut that door on God.

But in addition to the above named choices, there are other things that I know I had no control over. I wasn't consciously in control of the fact that I suddenly found myself missing God and grieving for Him. That feeling snuck up on me totally unawares. I also had no control over what people preached in the sermons I heard while I was away from God. At times these preachers stimulated my thoughts a lot. Most importantly of all I was blessed by the people I met.

I eventually told my friend Elsa and one or two people

at her church about my lack of faith. Elsa remained the true friend she has always been. She and her friends prayed for me once or twice when I visited. I didn't find being prayed for easy but they were so kind. They showed their concern without being judgmental. They loved me. They treated me with grace. I thank God for the blessing they have been to me.

Before I moved to Peacehaven I had searched for local churches online. In this way, I found Coastlands church before I moved here and I got in touch via Facebook. It was through the Coastlands Church Facebook page that I found myself in touch with Wendy Wilkinson. Wendy was a huge blessing to me in the months I was away from God. She was so welcoming to me even though at first I didn't attend Coastlands but went to the Church of the Ascension. The first time I met her I got a huge welcoming hug. She never judged me for falling away from God – not once. She simply loved me to the best of her ability. She allowed me to talk to her and she didn't force me to believe anything. At first, she didn't offer to pray with me, although I am certain she was praying for me when I wasn't with her. If she had wanted to pray for me while I was actually there it would have freaked me out and likely would have made my return even less likely. Very wisely she only prayed for me when I was ready for it. She also didn't lecture me on things about God or the Bible. She respected my training and previous knowledge of God.

Recently, I came to understand the role Wendy played even more, after I read 'Bringing home the Prodigals' by

Rob Parsons[22]. This book is a valuable look at the issue of people not just leaving church but walking away from God as I did. The story of the Prodigal Son is one that Jesus told and it is recorded in the fifteenth chapter of Luke's gospel. The elder brother in the story was judgmental when his brother returned from his wanderings. His first instinct was to criticize the prodigal for walking away from the father and wasting his money. The father's reaction was to run towards his son as soon as he saw him, throw his arms around him and throw a huge party.

Wendy's reaction to me was like of the father from the story. I was greatly blessed that one of the first people I met and told my story to reacted like the father and not the elder brother. The way Rob Parsons describes it is to say that we should always leave a light on for the prodigals. I pray God blesses Wendy for the way she left a light on for me.

I am also blessed by the people I didn't meet as well. I was fortunate not to come across any 'elder brothers'. I never met anyone who was judgmental about my wandering away from God. Mind you, I was very careful whom I told about it because I have met 'elder brothers' before. If I am honest I have been one before; I have judged others unfairly. I knew without a shadow of doubt that meeting an elder brother figure of any kind would send me scuttling away to the atheist camp really quickly. In his book, Rob Parsons wisely says that if our prodigals

---

22 Rob Parsons 'Bringing Home the Prodigals' is published by Hodder & Stoughton ISBN 0340861150.

come home then we should pray that they meet the father first and not the elder brother. He is so right. Meeting the elder brother type of person first is hugely damaging to a person who is a prodigal considering coming home again to God. The following verses are from Hosea 11:3-4 and they speak of God's reaction to a people who had turned their back on Him.

"It was I who taught Ephraim to walk, taking them by the arms; but they did not realize it was I who healed them. I led them with cords of human kindness, with ties of love; I lifted the yoke from their neck and bent down to feed them."

God is a God of love. We are told in Scripture that He is slow to anger and swift to love. It is good to remember how wise God is and try to emulate Him as best we can. If you know any prodigals love them first and foremost. Don't judge them because you are very likely making it harder for them to return.

When I began to write this chapter I couldn't work out why I came back to faith. I had a huge 'Why me' question permanently in my mind. Now I have written some of it I am beginning to see some of the reasons why I came back. As is often the case it was a variety of things. I hope that my story can help both others in the same situation and/or help those that know them. From what I can see at the moment the following things are the main contributory factors to my return to God.

1. Choosing to continue to go to Church sometimes. I didn't close the door on God completely.

2. My missing God and grieving for Him gave me the

incentive to seek Him seriously.

3. A willingness to be as open as I could to the truth and not simply justify my existing position.

4. My Church Army training enabling me to look at my situation from as many angles as possible.

5. Having someone like Wendy acting as father figure to me, waiting patiently for my return with love and not judgment.

6. I didn't meet any 'elder brothers'.

For further discussion on this subject I highly recommend that you read the Rob Parsons book 'Bringing Home the Prodigals'. It is a really helpful book for anyone wanting to know more about this topic. I have worked out now that there are a variety of reasons why I came back to God and I am eternally grateful that I found faith again. In Matthew 24:10-14 Jesus says,

"At that time many will turn away from the faith and will betray and hate each other, and many false prophets will appear and deceive many people. Because of the increase of wickedness, the love of most will grow cold, but the one who stands firm to the end will be saved. And this gospel of the kingdom will be preached in the whole world as a testimony to all nations, and then the end will come."

I realize now how close I came to being one of those who 'turn away from the faith', whose love 'will grow cold'. I am thankful for the seemingly small decisions I made that encouraged my return to faith in God. More importantly, I am eternally grateful for all those people along the way who made my return that bit easier by 'leaving a light on'. But more than any thing else I am grateful to God. He was always there. He never stopped waiting for me to return. Behind all the reasons I have outlined above was God drawing me with cords of loving kindness. He is the real reason I have come back to faith. I thank Him now and for all eternity for His constant loving presence.

The other 'Why me?' question I had after coming back to faith follows on from the last one. I now want to know more clearly why I stopped believing in God in the first place. Also, what, if anything, could I have done to stop the descent into unbelief? Was it inevitable?

There are two main reasons I fell away from God. One of the main reasons I fell away was due to the immense pain and grief at not being married and becoming a mother. Giving up the lifelong dream of having children was a grief I found almost impossible to deal with. I have an unhelpful tendency to try to be too emotionally independent. By that I mean that I try to deal with everything on my own rather than sharing it with others. I'll readily share my thoughts about things but opening up my painful emotions to others was somewhat alien to me. When I did share the hurt I didn't always find help so I kept it to myself. Bottling up the pain and grief like that was unwise to say the least. I am now learning to be less independent when it comes to my emotions. My experience dealing with this grief makes me want to speak out about it so as to help others going through the same thing I did.

The other main reason for my unbelief was because I didn't tell anyone about my doubts. I kept them to myself predominantly because of my job as a parish evangelist. I've already said in earlier chapters that fear of change was a big part of my decision to keep quiet about my faith disintegrating. As a lay minister of religion my whole livelihood and home was dependant on my having a faith to share. Fear of losing my home and having to face a major relocation was the main reason why I didn't tell anyone. But that fear wasn't the only reason.

There was also an element of shame at my doubting God. I had been a Christian for twenty seven years when my crisis started and having to admit to such doubts was hard. However, as a minister of religion, it felt even harder. I had been to Church Army training college. I was the one who was supposed to have all the answers. I was meant to be leading others to faith and there I was gradually sinking into total unbelief. I was so embarrassed that I couldn't bring myself to tell anyone. I wanted to run away and hide. I was scared of their reaction to me. I thought I would be judged and condemned (that pesky 'elder brother' was rearing his head without even being there in the flesh).

I also didn't want to be responsible for causing anyone else to doubt if I shared what I was thinking about God. A part of that was me trying hard to avoid sharing my doubts by putting a 'holier than thou' attitude over them. A part of it was a genuine concern that I would bring someone down. Nevertheless, I should have shared my pain and my doubts with a trusted person. Looking back I should have told Matt my vicar at the time. He is such a loving and non-judgmental person that I could have trusted him with what was happening. I now know he would have helped in every way he could and would have stood by me as an employee as much as he could. I wish I had told him because it may have prevented many months of pain later.

If I could make one plea to the church it is that we develop honest and supportive relationships with each other that are based on reality and above all based on love. We need each other as we seek to follow God. If you are going through a hard time I beg you to seek out a trusted person with whom to share if it is at all possible. Paul tells us in Ephesians 6:2-5,

"Carry each other's burdens, and in this way you will fulfill the law of Christ. If anyone thinks he is something when he is nothing, he deceives himself. Each one should test his own actions. Then he can take pride in himself, without comparing himself to somebody else, for each one should carry his own load."

At first reading, these verses sound to me like they are contradicting themselves. Should we carry one another's burdens or should we carry our own load? I believe Paul is saying that we are responsible for our own loads but part of being responsible load-bearers is to allow others to help us carry them. We have to allow others to come alongside us and help us with what seems too heavy a burden to bear. Sometimes we have to ask for help. Other people don't always see through the superficial masks we so often wear in church. We have to tell them what is going on underneath that mask. We need to be real with each other. I didn't do that. I was full of pride that I could do it alone for whatever reason. I paid the price for that. I hope that some of you will learn from my life experience. I pray you will be responsible load bearers and allow others to bear your burden with you. Praise God He brought me back to Himself despite the pride, fear, and shame that kept me silent about my difficulties.

20

Being not doing

Since my return to faith, as I stated in previous chapters, I've found that my faith is different than it was before. It's less focused on what I do, and who I am, and more focused on who God is, and what He has already done through Jesus. It feels much healthier this way. Prior to my crisis of faith I found it so easy to turn what is supposed to be salvation by faith into salvation by works. I am sure I am not the only person to experience this by a long way. For so long I had misconceptions about what a 'good' Christian is. I had a list of unhelpful rules in my head that I should follow if I were to be a 'proper' Christian. Do any of my rules ring bells with you? Do you believe any of them for yourself? The rules might be that being a 'good' Christian means . . .

I must believe the right things.

I must go to Church every Sunday at least once.

I must go to at least one midweek Bible study.

I must have my own 'quiet time' by reading my Bible and praying for at least half an hour every morning.

I must tithe my income.

I must try to share my faith with at least one person this week.

I must . . .

When does this stop? When do I just sit and be with God with no agenda? When do I realize that being a Christian isn't about what I have done – either good or bad. It is about what God has done. It about the fact that Jesus died so that the unhelpful and sinful things I have done are washed away and considered irrelevant by God. He died to give me a new start. His love is overwhelming and transforming. Why then would I want to live by a long list of musts, oughts, and shoulds? Why would I want to turn this amazing faith of grace into a religion of works once more?

I am not saying that any of the things on the above list are wrong. They are clearly all good in themselves. What I am challenging is the idea that following these rules is what makes us a Christian. Having a list like this in my mind made me feel that it was what I did that made me a Christian but that is wrong, so wrong. It is believing in God and His unending mercy, believing in His redeeming love in action by sending His son to die for me that makes me a Christian. All I do is accept this truth. The things on that list are things I aim to do out of gratitude that I am a Christian. They are things I do in order to show love for God but they do not make me a Christian in and of themselves.

When I look back to my faith before this crisis I see someone who talked about salvation by faith but who lived a salvation by works. I spent a lot of time trying to earn God's favor. Once I realized this I started to ask myself why I became an evangelist in the first place. It may not have been solely because I had noble aims of 'reaching the lost', or wanting to 'introduce people to Jesus'. I think to a large extent I was trying to earn God's favor. Although I would be untrue to myself if I said it was all misplaced motives.

At least a part of me was responding to a call from God to be involved in full time ministry of some kind. As previously mentioned I'd spent much of my nursing career terrified that God would ask me to go to some developing country where it is really hot and they have scary creepy crawlies. When the call came to minister to the people of Britain I was hugely relieved! My view of God at the time was 'if you dread doing something, then that is always what He will make you do'. I remember being challenged and hopeful at the same time, when I read something written by Gerald Coates, which said my ministry would likely be something I enjoyed doing.

It was the first time I had seriously considered that maybe God would not make me do the very thing I dreaded. It also made me think that Gerald Coates knew a different God to the one I knew at the time. Thankfully I'm now getting to know this 'new' God as well!

On the surface, I was feeling holy because of my choice of career. I wanted to serve God. A part of me was proud of the fact that I wanted to do these things with my life. That in itself was a somewhat bad start to the career! St Paul tells us in 1 Corinthians 10:12,

"So, if you think you are standing firm, be careful that you don't fall!"

They are wise words indeed. The more I thought about this in the weeks that followed my return to faith, the more I realized I was trying to earn favor from God by becoming an evangelist. In fact, I was trying to do more than that. I had been trying to earn a husband and children.

On the surface I was saying all the right things about why I was in ministry. However, underneath it all was a little girl desperately trying to earn love from her heavenly Father so that He would give her what she wanted. I was trying to prove to myself and to God that I am loveable. I was, in effect, believing that Jesus dying on the cross didn't prove that God loves me. I believed I needed more proof. Not the best start to an evangelistic ministry.

I've become aware now that much (but not all) of my understanding of God was head knowledge not heart knowledge. I could say the right things and I could teach others the right things. I taught about the grace of God and about His unconditional love and acceptance. However, at a heart level, I was still trying to earn His love and acceptance by being a 'good girl' and thereby earn the life I wanted. I knew I was saved because I had repented and given my life to the Lord Jesus but my sense of the love of God for me was warped. It's almost as if I was trying to experience the love of God vicariously by leading others to His love but I wasn't experiencing it myself a lot of the time.

Obedience should be a reaction of gratitude to God's grace, to His love poured out into our hearts by the Holy Spirit. It is not a way of earning His love and blessings. John 14:23-24 says,

"Jesus replied, "Anyone who loves me will obey my teaching. My Father will love them, and we will come to them and make our home with them. Anyone who does

not love me will not obey my teaching. These words you hear are not my* own; they belong to the Father who sent me."

When I read that verse, I used to see in my mind an angry God wagging his finger at me, saying petulantly 'if you loved me, you would obey me'. I read that verse as if God was saying 'you say you love me, well prove it by doing as you're told!' I received those verses as if they were from a bad-tempered God, who was trying to emotionally blackmail me into obedience.

Now I see those verses in a different light. I am beginning to realize what Jesus is saying. I personally believe He is saying, 'It is your love for me that will give you the ability to obey me'. The more we love someone the easier it is to do things for them. The love we feel for them motivates us to do things that please them. It motivates us to make sacrifices for them. Obeying Jesus' teaching is the same. The more we love Him the more we will automatically want to obey Him. And how do we grow to love God? Well, I have always loved the verse from 1 John 4:19,

"We love because He first loved us."

The key to us loving God more is to be more aware of how much He loves us first.

One of my favorite stories of the life of Jesus is the description of how he dealt with the woman caught in adultery. As Jesus was teaching in the synagogue one day the Pharisees and teachers of the law brought to him a woman who was caught in the act of adultery. I wonder what they did to the man who would have been with her for her to be 'caught in the act'. He appears to have got away with it completely. The woman's acusers reminded Jesus that the Law of Moses commanded that she be stoned to death and they wanted to know what he thought. They wanted to trap him into giving a wrong answer. If he said 'stone her' then he would be disobeying the Roman authorities who forbade the Jews giving out the death sentence. If he set her free, he was denying the Law of Moses. The Pharisees thought they had given him a catch 22 situation. At first, Jesus bent down and wrote in the sand. I have to be honest and say if I were that woman waiting there for the verdict I would be angry at seeing Jesus delay answering them! After continued questioning by the leaders, he said,

"Let any one of you who is without sin be the first to throw a stone at her."[23]

I love Jesus' response for a variety of reasons. Firstly, he foils the trap set for him by the religious leaders because he neither puts her to death nor disregards the Law of Moses. Secondly, he makes sure that she is set free. He shows immense love to this woman. It is only after he has forgiven her, after he has shown her love, that he says to her 'Go and sin no more'. The love and forgiveness came first. Then the 'Go and sin no more'. In that order. The love. The forgiveness. Then the 'Go and sin no more'. I knew that but still I would live as though Jesus was saying, 'Go and sin no more, then confess loads of times, then and only then, will I forgive you so I can love you'. Incidentally,

---

[23] This story is found in John 7: 53 – 8:11

He Never Let Go

it's interesting that Jesus doesn't get a confession out of her first. He simply jumps in with the forgiveness. That in itself is a challenge to the idea of a God who needs to hear a confession or He won't forgive you, isn't it? He saw her sin and he forgave her. She didn't have to earn it in any way whatsoever. I think God is far more merciful and loving than we ever give Him credit for. No, I don't think, I know God is far more merciful and loving than most of us give Him credit for.

21

Love and freedom

By this stage in my return to faith I was realizing more and more I needed to experience God at a heart level not just a head level. Intellectually I knew God loved me but my heart didn't really feel loved by Him. I now knew I had to receive the Father's love. I needed to open my heart to Him and let Him love me. I knew instinctively this was going to be far more important in my future walk with Him than anything else. I wanted to open my heart to Him but fear stopped me. I had spent a lot of my time in ministry receiving things about God at a head level, and then immediately giving them away by telling others the same thing. In this way I didn't have to let it drop into my heart. I now knew I didn't want to do that anymore. I wanted to start receiving the things I learn about God into my heart - it is the only way to freedom. And I knew I needed freedom from things holding me back in my life such as the food addiction.

I started praying about my need to open up my heart to God's love. I prayed often. I wanted to open up to God's love but somehow I was too scared to do it. I kept pushing Him away and over eating to fill up the emptiness. I don't know why but fear had too strong a grip around my heart for me to open my heart to Him. I didn't know what to do.

He Never Let Go

I ended up really sobbing about it before the Lord. I begged Him to help me.

"I know I need to open up my heart to your love Lord, but I don't know how to do it. Please help me I just don't know how to let you into my heart."

Not knowing how to open up to God scared me. If I didn't know how to go about it, how could I actually do it? There was a sense of panic in my heart as I realized I was trapped into a corner. I knew I had to open up to God's love if I was seriously going to move forward in my life with Jesus. But at the same time, I was terrified of doing it. I didn't know how to overcome the fear and I didn't know how to hand the fear over to God.

Once again, God stepped into my life in an amazing way to sort this one out for me. I think He knew the genuine cry of His child in her dilemma. God answered my prayer in an unexpected way. I had a dream one night not long after I had begged God to help me in opening up to Him. I dreamed I was leaving to go on a journey somewhere with friends. I don't know where we were going but preparations for leaving on the trip were taking up all our attention. Our luggage was being packed into a campervan before we set off on what I was sure was going to be a very exciting journey. Unexpectedly, just as we were about to leave, I noticed Jesus stood in the corner of the garage with a look of immeasurable love on his face. I felt totally, utterly and completely overwhelmed by this love. I felt his love at a deep and life affirming heart level. I knew without a doubt that Jesus had been standing there the whole time. He had been standing there watching as my friends and I ran around getting ready for our trip but we had been completely ignoring him. Then I knew beyond all shadow of doubt that I couldn't leave Jesus. There was no way I was going to walk away from a pure and total love like the love I knew he had for me. I rushed over to Jesus and like a child with her father I reached out and he hugged me. I awoke from this powerful dream still feeling this love, and it has stayed with me. I knew when I awoke that God had been with me in my crisis of faith the whole time. He never once let me go. He stayed close just waiting for my return. I felt as if I had been 'born again' again!

The artist Charlie Mackesy[24] has done a series of paintings, sketches, and sculptures around the theme of the prodigal son/daughter. The picture on the front cover of this book is a painting by Charlie called 'Sketch for the prodigal daughter'. There is another one of his pictures hanging on my wall (actually it's a framed postcard) called 'The Prodigal Daughter'. Both of these paintings show a woman being held in Jesus' loving arms despite having run away from Him, and rejected Him. Jesus is cradling this runaway daughter with immense love.

I was like that prodigal daughter. I had run away from Jesus. I had totally rejected God and Jesus, but Jesus scooped me up into His arms and hugged me anyway. The blue drizzle behind the characters in the picture on the front cover of the book speaks to me about Jesus rescuing me from tears and brokenness. I was blown away (and I still am) by the fact that Jesus just waited quietly until I

---

24 Go to www.charliemackesy.com to see Charlie's stunning work.

He Never Let Go

noticed Him. He just went on loving me. I finally know at a deeper heart level than I have ever known before that I am loved by God. I put my copy of 'The Prodigal Daughter' up on the wall near the door so that every time I leave my apartment I am reminded of how much God loves me. He loves me unconditionally. He loves you the same way, whoever you are, whatever you have done.

It is so sad that I used to live my life as if God were looking for an excuse to reject me. This couldn't be further from the truth. A God who sends His own Son to die for us isn't looking an excuse to reject me. He is looking for an excuse to run to me and throw His arms of love around me and welcome me home again.

This experience of Jesus' love took me on a journey to discover the love of God as Father. I spent time reading about God's Fatherhood and what it means to us. The more I read the more I realized this is what my heart was really seeking. I needed to know God's love as Father. A lot of my relationship with God was with Jesus, as a King, friend and brother. I didn't relate to God as a Father. But now I recognized this is what I really needed. I got to the stage where my need to know more about the Father love of God consumed me. I found myself praying "Lord, I don't care if I am a fat food addict for the rest of my life, I just want to know you and your Father love" And I meant it. I had stopped seeking healing for my addiction and started to simply seek Father. I was seeking the Healer not the healing. I just wanted Him and nothing else.

My discovery of the love of Father God at this deeper heart level had the most amazing outcome. I gradually realized that I was gradually trusting God more all the time. I mean trusting Him with the parts of me that I often kept hidden, the parts I buried in food.

One Sunday morning in March 2012 I woke up feeling that something was in the air, something was different but I couldn't quite put my finger on what was happening. I put it down to the fact that my friend Wendy, of whom I have already spoken, was coming back to our church to preach. She had moved away from our town to be nearer children and grandchildren. I was really looking forward to seeing her again.

The service went well and I felt very close to God during it. As it progressed I became increasingly aware I was ready to lay down my eating disorder. I had spent years searching for freedom but now I realized I simply needed to lay it down. It was my decision to allow God to put to death the addiction. I no longer needed it. I had God as Father and He was taking the place of food as a place of refuge. God would free me but I had to allow Him to do so and up until now I would not let Him do it. I had spent years thinking He was stopping me be free but now I knew the truth that I was stopping myself. I knew I needed to pray myself about this but I wanted to do it in the presence of a strong and trusted Christian friend. And this is where Wendy came in. The end of the service came and I went up to Wendy and asked her to pray with me.

I stood in front of her, butterflies of anticipation and excitement fluttering in my stomach. I honestly can't remember now what I prayed and what Wendy prayed. I do know I asked God to take the place of food in my life and I told him I wanted to lay it down. Wendy also prayed for me, standing with me in my request for freedom. Wendy still remembers some of the words she prayed that day. God gave them to her during the service before she knew I would come and ask her to pray with me. She said,

"Today Lynda, is the first day of the rest of your life, a new beginning, STEP OUT"

And that is what happened. I stepped out, away from food addiction and into freedom with God holding my hand and Wendy praying for me each moment. I was free. I knew I was free. I felt different. I felt a burden lifted from me. I was no longer a compulsive overeater[25].

The following weeks were amazing as I realized how free I now was. I no longer wanted to binge all the time. I ate when I was hungry and stopped when I was full. There were times when I was very emotional and I felt the urge to overeat. But if I started towards the kitchen I knew I wasn't hungry and couldn't eat.

To this day I have not binged. The worst that happens is choosing rubbish food when I am both emotional and hungry. But still when I am full I stop eating. I am like everyone else. I will overeat normally at Christmas and other holidays but then go back to normal. Four years after I was freed from food addiction I have lost 55lbs in weight. It is coming off very gradually and it is staying off. I still have a lot to lose as I was almost double

---

[25] If you would like to know more about my journey to freedom from food addiction you can read it in my book, *Being Known: My journey to freedom from food addiction.* Available from Amazon in paperback and on Kindle

the weight I should be when God freed me. But I would rather keep on losing weight slowly and know it is coming off permanently.

As I write this chapter I remember Isaiah 62:1-5, which was prophesied over me in 1989 while I was attending Bible College at Roffey Place in Horsham.

"For Zion's sake I will not keep silent, for Jerusalem's sake I will not remain quiet, till her vindication shines out like the dawn, her salvation like a blazing torch. The nations will see your vindication, and all kings your glory; you will be called by a new name that the mouth of the LORD will bestow. You will be a crown of splendor in the LORD's hand, a royal diadem in the hand of your God. No longer will they call you Deserted, or name your land Desolate. But you will be called Hephzibah, and your land Beulah, for the LORD will take delight in you, and your land will be married. As a young man marries a young woman, so will your Builder marry you; as a bridegroom rejoices over his bride, so will your God rejoice over you."

I am beginning to see the truth of these words in my life now more than I have ever done. I still have a long way to go before they are a complete reality in my life (probably not until I get to heaven to be honest) but I am so much further now I have ever been. These words tell me God is speaking, and not keeping silent on my behalf. He is leading me onwards towards the goal of righteousness. His words to me are words of love. They encourage me on the road to righteousness. When I get to heaven my path to righteousness will be complete but for now I am happy to be working with God as we walk down the path together.

He Never Let Go

I was delighted when I preached at Christ Church Turnham Green on Friday 23rd March 2012 and again on Sunday 25th March 2012. It was a very healing experience because the last time I had preached anywhere before 23rd March 2012 was at Christ Church Turnham Green at the carol service I describe at the beginning of this book. Their current vicar Richard even prayed that it would be a re-commissioning for me. I have no doubt that my ministry will be stronger because of what I have come through over the last couple of years. I have started to really miss being in ministry. I realize now that the call on my life to work for Jesus in this way has not gone away, it was just hibernating over winter! But praise God the spring is coming and my ministry gifts will be used once more.

I can see now that God is already gently restoring my ministry. Such grace! I have taken studies at my home group again and have enjoyed it. I have had the opportunity to speak to the ladies group at our church and also at St Aldate's in Oxford and I am on the preaching rota for services at my church on a Sunday.

Now I have come out the other side of such a major crisis of faith I can say that God has used it to bring about much needed change in my view of Him. My faith is far more God centered and less Church centered. Church is now in its rightful place of supporting role. Father, Son and Holy Spirit are number one. I've learned about faith, doubt, and certainty. I have learned that certainty is the enemy of real faith. I have learned that real faith lives alongside the questions and doubts. I have learned that my experience of a crisis of faith has actually had the long term effect of deepening my faith not diminishing it. I've learned that God can speak to me powerfully in dreams. I've learned about God's love for me and I've experienced God's love for me at a heart level. As a direct consequence of that love I have learned to live in freedom from food addiction.

I've learned the necessity of allowing God into my pain and sharing my pain with others. I've learned there are people out there who are willing to sit with you as you pour out your pain. I'm still learning I need to be less emotionally independent. I'm learning to give my pain to God and ask Him to use it for His glory. I've experienced people showing me the love of God in simply waiting for me to return to Him. I've learned the importance of not allowing anything to get in the way of my relationship with God, not even the church. I am learning to let go of salvation by works and replace it with salvation by grace. I've discovered that grace, the immense grace and mercy of God in a way I have never done before.

But most of all I have learned one thing above all else. And it is a lesson I hope you can learn without going through what I did. I have learned that no matter what happens, no matter what I say or what I do there is one thing about God that I trust absolutely. God will always have His hand on my life. Yes now I know for sure. He never lets go.

Also by this author

"A must read for anyone struggling with an addiction. Through it all Lynda points to the source of her healing, the Lord Jesus Christ, giving Him the glory. Brilliant!"*

"Food is an anesthetic and its anaesthetizing powers have me imprisoned"
Lynda Alsford was a captive who dreamed of freedom from addictive overeating.

"I had a hole in me somewhere... a black hole of pain sucking in all the food around me"
Would she ever work out how to fill the hole in her soul with something other than food?

Being Known describes Lynda's long, arduous journey to find freedom from addiction to food. Share her triumphs and disappointments over many years of searching as she edged her way to freedom through Jesus.

Available on Kindle from Amazon and in paperback from Amazon, www.lulu.com and www.lyndaalsford.com

"A book of hope for anyone dealing with an eating addiction....She writes with honesty ... Lynda opens her heart and shares a journey that at times has been difficult. ...Well worth buying. It could be a precious first step in finding your own healing"*.

*Both quotes are from different 5 star reviews on Amazon

About the author

I live near the sea in East Sussex, which I love. Being a short walking distance from the cliff tops is wonderful. I wish I had moved to here much sooner. It's lovely, although it is also somewhat windy!

I live with my 3 legged rescue cat Sir Charles Limpalot. Charlie (as he's known to his friends) is proud, and doesn't consider himself disabled by his missing front left paw. He likes belly rubs, and occasionally bringing me live frogs, birds and mice as presents. I do not like these presents.

I enjoy getting lost in a good book and belong to a couple of local book groups. I have also begun to paint recently although I am definitely still a total beginner.

I write a monthly email newsletter called *Seeking the Healer*, which gives encouragement to those seeking to discover freedom and more of God in their lives. Sign up for it at my website www.lyndaalsford.com

I am available for talks/presentations about any of the issues in this book, such as experiencing a crisis of faith, unwanted singleness or a need to experience more of God's love. If you are interested in booking a talk please contact me by email on lynda@lyndaalsford.com.

God bless you

Lynda

www.lyndaalsford.com